The Historical Forensic Files: Unsolved Cases Through Time

Shah Rukh

Published by Shah Rukh, 2024.

THE HISTORICAL FORENSIC FILES: UNSOLVED CASES THROUGH TIME

First edition. July 31, 2024.

Written by Shah Rukh.

Table of Contents

Prologue

In every era, from the ancient to the modern, humanity has been haunted by mysteries that defy explanation, events that leave behind more questions than answers. These are not the tales of fictional intrigue but real-life puzzles that have eluded the most skilled investigators, the brightest minds, and the most advanced technologies. They are the echoes of the unsolved, resonating through history, reminding us of the limits of our understanding.

In "The Historical Forensic Files: Unsolved Cases Through Time," we embark on a journey across the centuries, exploring the most perplexing and enigmatic cases that remain shrouded in mystery. From the eerie shadows of Victorian London, where Jack the Ripper's identity remains a secret, to the chilling waters off California, where the actress Natalie Wood met a tragic and unresolved end, these stories span the globe and the spectrum of human experience.

Each chapter is a window into a moment of fear, confusion, and uncertainty, a snapshot of a world grappling with the unknown. Some cases are marked by the brutality of a killer's hand, others by the sudden disappearance of a person or a group, leaving behind a void that no amount of searching could fill. In these pages, we find not just stories of crime and loss, but also the broader human quest for understanding and closure.

What is it about these cases that fascinates and unnerves us? Perhaps it is the realization that, despite our advancements, some truths remain just out of reach, hidden in the mists of time or the shadows of our own nature. These unsolved mysteries challenge our perceptions of justice and reality, reminding us that not all stories have clear endings.

As we delve into these historical forensic files, we must confront the uncomfortable truth that not every question has an answer, not every mystery a resolution. Yet, it is in the pursuit of these answers, in the relentless quest to uncover the truth, that we find a reflection of our own fears, hopes, and the eternal human desire to make sense of the world.

So, let us begin this journey through the annals of the unexplained, where each chapter serves as a testament to the enduring mysteries that continue to captivate and perplex. These are the stories that have puzzled experts, baffled investigators, and haunted the public imagination—stories that, despite the passage of time, remain stubbornly unsolved.

Chapter 1: The Enigmatic Death of Elisa Lam

The case of Elisa Lam is one of the most puzzling and mysterious incidents in recent history, often attracting widespread interest and speculation. Elisa Lam was a 21-year-old Canadian student who tragically died under mysterious circumstances in 2013. Her body was discovered in a water tank on the roof of the Cecil Hotel in Los Angeles, California, weeks after she had been reported missing. The circumstances surrounding her death, combined with bizarre video footage and the eerie history of the hotel, have made this case a focal point for conspiracy theories and intense public scrutiny.

Elisa Lam was last seen alive on January 31, 2013. She was staying at the Cecil Hotel, a place known for its history of crime and strange occurrences, including connections to infamous serial killers like Richard Ramirez, also known as the "Night Stalker." Lam had been traveling alone as part of a trip through the United States, documenting her journey on social media and keeping in touch with her family. However, on the day she was supposed to check out of the hotel, she disappeared.

The case gained widespread attention when the Los Angeles Police Department released a surveillance video from the hotel's elevator. The footage showed Lam behaving in an inexplicably strange manner. She was seen entering the elevator, pressing several buttons, then standing in the corner of the elevator as if she were hiding. At various points, she exited the elevator, peered around the corner, and gestured as if talking to someone out of view. Her movements appeared erratic and confused, leading to a myriad of interpretations and theories about what might have been happening.

The video quickly went viral, and speculation ran rampant. Many viewers speculated that Lam was under the influence of drugs or suffering from a mental health crisis. However, the toxicology report later revealed that she had no illegal drugs in her system at the time of her death, though it did indicate that she had not been taking her prescribed medication for bipolar disorder consistently. This finding led to further speculation that Lam might have been experiencing a manic episode, which could explain her unusual behavior.

The mystery deepened when, on February 19, 2013, Lam's body was found in one of the hotel's water tanks. The discovery was made after guests complained about low water pressure and an unusual taste in the water. Maintenance workers investigating the complaint found Lam's body submerged in the tank. The circumstances of her death were puzzling: the tanks were located on the roof of the hotel, a restricted area requiring a key and passcode to access. The lids of the tanks were heavy and difficult to move, raising questions about how Lam could have accessed the tanks and ended up inside.

The official cause of death was determined to be accidental drowning, with bipolar disorder cited as a significant condition contributing to her death. However, the lack of clear evidence and the bizarre circumstances led to numerous alternative theories. Some speculated that Lam was murdered, possibly by someone with access to the restricted areas of the hotel. Others suggested more supernatural explanations, citing the hotel's dark history and the unsettling nature of the elevator video.

The case also brought attention to the Cecil Hotel itself, which has a long and eerie history. The hotel has been associated with numerous suicides, overdoses, and other violent incidents over the years. It was once home to Elizabeth Short, the infamous "Black Dahlia," shortly before her murder in 1947. The hotel's dark past and the unexplained nature of Lam's death have fueled a mythology around the location, making it a subject of fascination and fear.

Despite extensive investigation, many questions remain unanswered. How did Lam access the restricted rooftop area? Why did she enter the water tank, and was she alone at the time? The lack of concrete answers has led to continued speculation and interest in the case. Some people believe that the case involves foul play or supernatural elements, while others see it as a tragic outcome of mental illness.

The case has had a significant cultural impact, inspiring documentaries, podcasts, and countless online discussions. It serves as a reminder of the often-unpredictable nature of mental illness and the tragic outcomes that can arise when someone in crisis goes unnoticed or unsupported. Additionally, it highlights the importance of mental health awareness and the need for better systems to support individuals struggling with mental health issues.

In the years since Lam's death, the case has continued to capture the public's imagination. It has been the subject of numerous analyses, with internet sleuths poring over every detail, searching for clues that might provide a definitive answer. The elevator video, in particular, remains a source of fascination and debate, with each gesture and movement scrutinized for meaning.

Ultimately, the case of Elisa Lam is a complex and tragic story that touches on issues of mental health, the power of the internet in shaping public perception, and the mysteries that sometimes surround unexplained deaths. While some may find the official explanation sufficient, others continue to seek answers, driven by the eerie circumstances and the lingering questions that remain. The case remains unsolved in the minds of many, a modern-day enigma that continues to captivate and intrigue people around the world.

Chapter 2: The Mystery of the Hinterkaifeck Murders

The Hinterkaifeck murders are one of the most perplexing and chilling unsolved cases in German history, a crime that has baffled investigators and intrigued the public for nearly a century. The case involves the gruesome killings of six people at a remote farmstead called Hinterkaifeck, located near the town of Gröbern in Bavaria, Germany. On the night of March 31, 1922, an unknown assailant or assailants brutally murdered the entire Gruber family and their maid. The victims included Andreas Gruber, 63; his wife, Cäzilia, 72; their widowed daughter Viktoria Gabriel, 35; Viktoria's children, Cäzilia, 7, and Josef, 2; and the maid, Maria Baumgartner, 44, who had only recently started working for the family.

The story of the Hinterkaifeck murders begins with a series of unsettling events that occurred in the days leading up to the crime. Andreas Gruber had reported hearing strange noises coming from the attic and finding footprints in the snow leading from the forest to the farm, but none leading back. Despite these ominous signs, the Grubers did not report anything to the authorities or seek help from neighbors. The farm was isolated, and the family was known to be somewhat reclusive, which may have contributed to their decision to handle the situation on their own.

The discovery of the crime itself was horrifying. A few days after the murders, neighbors became concerned when no one had seen the Gruber family and they had not attended church, which was unusual for them. Upon investigation, they found the bodies of Andreas, Cäzilia, Viktoria, and young Cäzilia in the barn, where they had been lured one by one and killed with a mattock, a type of agricultural tool. The maid Maria and the youngest child Josef were found inside the house. Maria was discovered in her bed, while Josef was found in his cot in Viktoria's room. All the victims had suffered severe head injuries, and it was apparent that the murders had been committed with great brutality.

One of the most disturbing aspects of the case is the behavior of the killer or killers after the murders. It appeared that the perpetrator had stayed at the farm for several days after the crime, feeding the livestock, eating meals from the family's pantry, and generally going about daily chores as if nothing had happened. This bizarre detail added to the horror and mystery of the case, suggesting a cold and calculating mind behind the killings.

The investigation into the murders was extensive but ultimately fruitless. Despite numerous theories and suspects, the case was never solved. Several individuals were interrogated, and some suspects even confessed under duress, but none of the confessions were considered reliable. Theories about the motive for the murders ranged from robbery to personal vendettas. Some speculated that the crimes were committed by someone close to the family, possibly even someone who had a key to the property, given the apparent lack of forced entry and the perpetrator's familiarity with the farm.

One of the more salacious theories revolved around the family itself, particularly the relationship between Andreas Gruber and his daughter Viktoria. It was rumored that Andreas and Viktoria had an incestuous relationship, and there was speculation that Josef was the product of this relationship. This theory was fueled by rumors and gossip in the local community, as well as by the fact that Viktoria had previously been widowed under mysterious circumstances. However, there was no concrete evidence to support these claims, and they remain speculative.

Over the years, various other theories have emerged, including the possibility that the murders were committed by a vagrant or a mentally ill person who wandered into the area. Some have suggested that Viktoria's previous lover, Karl Gabriel, who was reported to have died in World War I, might have actually survived and returned to commit the murders out of jealousy or rage. This theory, like many others, is based more on speculation than solid evidence.

The case has also been revisited several times by both professional investigators and amateur sleuths. In the 1980s, the police files were reopened, and modern forensic techniques were applied to the evidence. However, the case was so old that much of the original evidence had deteriorated, and no new conclusions could be drawn. The farm itself was demolished in 1923, which further complicated efforts to re-examine the crime scene.

The Hinterkaifeck murders have inspired numerous books, documentaries, and fictional adaptations. The case's enduring appeal lies in its combination of a gruesome and baffling crime, an isolated and atmospheric setting, and a wealth of unanswered questions. The eerie details, such as the killer remaining at the farm after the murders, the mysterious sounds heard in the days leading up to the crime, and the apparent lack of motive, all contribute to the sense of mystery.

Despite the passage of time and numerous attempts to solve the case, the Hinterkaifeck murders remain one of Germany's most infamous cold cases. The mystery is compounded by the fact that the perpetrator or perpetrators were never identified, leaving the motive and circumstances surrounding the crime shrouded in uncertainty. The lack of resolution has kept the case alive in the public imagination, fostering a legacy of speculation and intrigue that continues to this day.

The Hinterkaifeck murders are a chilling reminder of how little we sometimes know about the darkest corners of human behavior. The case encapsulates the fear of the unknown and the unsettling possibility that the truth might never be uncovered. It stands as a poignant example of the limitations of forensic science and criminal investigation in the face of complex and inscrutable human actions. As such, it remains a subject of fascination for those interested in true crime, history, and the enduring mysteries of the human condition.

Chapter 3: The Vanishing of the Sodder Children

The disappearance of the Sodder children is one of the most perplexing and enduring mysteries in American history, a case that has puzzled investigators and captivated the public for decades. The story begins on Christmas Eve, 1945, in Fayetteville, West Virginia, when a fire consumed the home of George and Jennie Sodder and their nine children. In the aftermath of the blaze, five of the Sodder children—Maurice, 14; Martha, 12; Louis, 9; Jennie, 8; and Betty, 5—were unaccounted for, and their remains were never found. The circumstances surrounding the fire, the conflicting evidence, and the Sodder family's persistent belief that their children might still be alive have kept this case in the public eye for nearly 80 years.

On the night of the fire, the Sodder family had celebrated Christmas Eve together. George and Jennie Sodder, along with nine of their ten children, were at home. The eldest son, Joe, was away, serving in the military. That night, after celebrating and exchanging gifts, Jennie allowed some of the children to stay up later than usual, playing with their new toys. George and Jennie retired to bed around midnight, leaving the children still awake. A series of unusual and suspicious events occurred in the hours leading up to the fire, which have fueled speculation and controversy over the years.

At around 12:30 a.m., Jennie was awakened by a strange phone call. The caller asked for someone Jennie did not know, and when she said they had the wrong number, she noticed the woman on the other end of the line laughing strangely. As she returned to bed, Jennie noticed that some lights were still on in the house, the curtains were not drawn, and the front door was unlocked, which was unusual. She assumed some of the children had forgotten to close up and turned off the lights and locked the door before going to bed.

Shortly thereafter, Jennie was again awakened, this time by the sound of something hitting the roof with a loud bang, followed by a rolling noise. She fell back asleep, but about half an hour later, she woke up to the smell of smoke. Upon investigation, Jennie discovered a fire had broken out in George's office, which was located near the children's bedrooms. She quickly woke George, and they attempted to save their children. However, the staircase was engulfed in flames, making it impossible to reach the children's bedrooms upstairs.

In a desperate attempt to rescue the children, George and the older boys tried various methods. George broke a window, cutting himself badly in the process, to re-enter the house but was unable to get through the flames. He attempted to climb to the upper floor using a ladder that was usually kept propped against the house, but the ladder was mysteriously missing. George then tried to pull one of his trucks up to the house to climb on top of it to reach the windows, but inexplicably, neither of the two trucks would start, despite having been in good working order the previous day. All these failures seemed highly unusual and led to suspicions that the fire and the events surrounding it were not purely accidental.

The fire department, hampered by wartime shortages and the fact that it was a volunteer force, did not arrive until several hours later, by which time the house had burned to the ground. When the flames were finally extinguished, there was no sign of the five missing children, nor were there any remains found in the ashes, which seemed odd given the intensity and duration of the fire. The local coroner's office issued death certificates for the children, attributing their deaths to suffocation and burning, but this did little to quell the doubts of George and Jennie Sodder.

In the aftermath of the fire, numerous strange and suspicious details emerged. For one, the telephone line to the house had been cut, not burned, suggesting deliberate tampering. Witnesses reported seeing a man with a ladder stealing a block and tackle from the property on the night of the fire. Furthermore, a telephone repairman who came to fix the lines after the fire found that they had been cut, not destroyed by the fire, and he noted that they had been cut about 14 feet off the ground, higher than a person could reach without a ladder. Another strange detail was that a woman claimed to have seen the missing children in a car while the fire was still burning, and another woman reported serving them breakfast at a tourist stop some 50 miles away.

One of the most enduring pieces of evidence that kept the case alive was a photograph sent to the Sodders in 1949, four years after the fire. It purportedly showed one of the missing children, Louis, as a grown man. The picture was accompanied by a cryptic note that read, "Louis Sodder. I love brother Frankie. Ilil Boys. A90132 or 35." The family hired a private investigator to follow up on the lead, but he disappeared and was never heard from again, adding another layer of mystery to the case.

Over the years, George and Jennie Sodder pursued every lead, contacted the FBI, and hired private investigators, but no conclusive evidence ever emerged. They believed their children had been kidnapped and that the fire was a cover-up. They theorized that someone who had a grudge against George, possibly related to his outspoken criticism of Italian dictator Benito Mussolini and his anti-fascist stance, might have been involved. George, an Italian immigrant, had a history of conflicts with other members of the local Italian-American community, and he had received threats in the weeks leading up to the fire.

Despite extensive searches and investigations, no credible evidence was ever found to support any theory conclusively. The Sodders placed a billboard along Route 16 near the site of the fire, offering a reward for information leading to the recovery of their children and displaying photographs of the five missing children, keeping the case in the public eye. Jennie Sodder continued to believe her children were alive and awaited their return until her death in 1989.

The mystery of the Sodder children remains unsolved, with numerous theories but no definitive answers. The case encapsulates a series of baffling inconsistencies and unanswered questions, such as why no remains were found, despite the house burning for hours; why the ladder was missing; why the trucks wouldn't start; and why there were multiple reports of the children being seen after the fire. The story of the Sodder family is not just a tale of a tragic fire and missing children; it is also a testament to the tenacity of a family that refused to accept a simple explanation and continued to seek the truth against all odds.

To this day, the disappearance of the Sodder children continues to fascinate true crime enthusiasts and armchair detectives. The case has inspired numerous articles, books, and documentaries, all attempting to piece together what happened on that fateful Christmas Eve. The lack of resolution has left the story open to interpretation and speculation, and it remains one of the most enigmatic and emotionally charged mysteries in American history.

Chapter 4: The Zodiac Killer's Cryptic Legacy

The Zodiac Killer is one of the most infamous and elusive serial killers in American history, known not only for his brutal murders but also for the cryptic letters and ciphers he sent to the press and police. Operating in Northern California during the late 1960s and early 1970s, the Zodiac Killer is confirmed to have killed at least five people, though he claimed to have murdered 37. The killer's taunting communication and enigmatic ciphers have made the case a subject of intense interest and speculation for decades, creating a chilling legacy that continues to captivate true crime enthusiasts, investigators, and codebreakers.

The Zodiac Killer's first confirmed attacks occurred in the summer of 1968. On December 20, 1968, high school students Betty Lou Jensen and David Faraday were shot and killed near Vallejo, California, while sitting in a car at a secluded spot-on Lake Herman Road. Less than seven months later, on July 4, 1969, Darlene Ferrin and Michael Mageau were shot while sitting in a parked car at the Blue Rock Springs Park in Vallejo. Ferrin died from her wounds, but Mageau survived, providing the first description of the attacker. He described the shooter as a white male, approximately 5 feet 8 inches tall, with a stocky build and light-colored hair.

The killer's next attack took place on September 27, 1969, at Lake Berryessa. Bryan Hartnell and Cecelia Shepard were relaxing near the lake when they were approached by a man wearing a hooded costume featuring a white crossed-circle symbol on his chest, which would later become the Zodiac's signature emblem. The attacker tied them up before stabbing them repeatedly. Hartnell survived the attack, but Shepard succumbed to her injuries two days later. Before leaving the scene, the killer drew the crossed-circle symbol on Hartnell's car door and wrote the dates of the attacks, along with a message taunting the police.

The Zodiac's final confirmed murder occurred on October 11, 1969, when he shot and killed cab driver Paul Stine in the Presidio Heights neighborhood of San Francisco. The killer took Stine's wallet, car keys, and a piece of his shirt, which he later sent to the San Francisco Chronicle along with another letter. This letter included a chilling detail: the Zodiac claimed that he would target school children next, causing widespread panic in the area.

What set the Zodiac Killer apart from other serial killers of the time was his penchant for communication. The Zodiac sent a series of letters and ciphers to various newspapers, including the San Francisco Chronicle, the San Francisco Examiner, and the Vallejo Times-Herald. These letters often began with "This is the Zodiac speaking," and they included a combination of taunts, cryptic messages, and claims of additional murders. The killer demanded that his ciphers be published on the front pages of the newspapers, threatening further violence if his demands were not met.

The first of these ciphers, sent in three parts to the aforementioned newspapers in August 1969, was a 408-symbol cryptogram that the Zodiac claimed contained his identity. It was solved by a high school teacher named Donald Harden and his wife, Bettye, just days after its publication. The solution revealed a chilling message: the killer expressed his pleasure in killing and his belief that his victims would serve him in the afterlife. However, the cipher did not reveal the killer's name, as he had promised.

A second cipher, the 340-character cryptogram sent to the San Francisco Chronicle in November 1969, remained unsolved for over 51 years. It was finally cracked in December 2020 by an international team of amateur codebreakers, including David Oranchak, Jarl Van Eycke, and Sam Blake. The message revealed in the cipher continued the Zodiac's taunts and did not provide his identity, only furthering the mystery.

Throughout his correspondence, the Zodiac Killer displayed a chilling sense of control and a desire for attention. He often taunted the police for their inability to catch him and mocked the public's fear. The Zodiac's letters also included references to various cultural symbols and literary works, such as Gilbert and Sullivan's "The Mikado," adding another layer of complexity to his messages. The use of the crossed-circle symbol, which became his signature, further cemented his identity as the Zodiac Killer and added a chilling iconography to his legacy.

One of the most enduring aspects of the Zodiac Killer case is the wide array of suspects and theories that have emerged over the years. Dozens of individuals have been considered potential suspects, with varying degrees of plausibility. One of the most well-known suspects is Arthur Leigh Allen, a Vallejo resident who was investigated extensively by the police. Allen had a history of sexual misconduct and was known to have an interest in young children, matching the Zodiac's threat to target school children. However, despite circumstantial evidence linking him to the crimes, including the fact that he wore a Zodiac brand wristwatch and made comments about shooting the tires of a school bus, no definitive evidence was found to connect him to the murders. Allen died in 1992, leaving his involvement in the case unresolved.

Another prominent suspect is Richard Gaikowski, a journalist and filmmaker who lived in the Bay Area during the time of the killings. Gaikowski was linked to the case by a former colleague who claimed that his voice matched the Zodiac's, as described by surviving victims. However, like many other suspects, there was no conclusive evidence to prove his guilt.

The case has also been the subject of numerous books, documentaries, and films, most notably David Fincher's 2007 film

"Zodiac," based on the book by Robert Graysmith. Graysmith, a former cartoonist for the San Francisco Chronicle, became obsessed with the case and spent years researching and writing about it. His books, "Zodiac" and "Zodiac Unmasked," popularized the case and introduced many theories and suspects to the public.

Despite the extensive investigation and the work of countless amateur sleuths, the Zodiac Killer has never been caught, and his true identity remains unknown. The case has become a symbol of the frustrations and limitations of criminal investigation, particularly in cases involving serial killers who are meticulous, calculating, and able to evade capture. The Zodiac's use of ciphers and cryptic messages has also drawn comparisons to other notorious figures in criminal history, such as Jack the Ripper, who similarly taunted the police and public through letters.

In addition to the ciphers and letters, the Zodiac case is notable for its influence on popular culture and its role in the development of criminal profiling. The killer's ability to instill fear, his taunting of the authorities, and his use of coded messages have inspired countless works of fiction, from films and television shows to novels and graphic novels. The case has also had a significant impact on the field of criminal profiling, with experts analyzing the Zodiac's behavior and writings to create psychological profiles that might help identify him.

The legacy of the Zodiac Killer is one of fear, mystery, and an enduring fascination with the unknown. The case remains one of the most famous unsolved serial killer cases in the world, and the mystery surrounding the killer's identity continues to intrigue and frustrate both amateur and professional investigators. The Zodiac Killer's cryptic messages, taunting letters, and chilling murders have left an indelible mark on the history of crime and have ensured that the case will continue to be studied and discussed for many years to come.

Chapter 5: The Disappearance of Amelia Earhart

The disappearance of Amelia Earhart is one of the most enduring mysteries of the 20th century, capturing the imagination of people worldwide. Earhart was a pioneering aviator and one of the most famous women of her time. Her disappearance during an attempt to circumnavigate the globe in 1937 has sparked countless theories, investigations, and enduring fascination. The case combines elements of adventure, mystery, and the uncharted frontiers of early aviation, making it a compelling story that continues to intrigue both scholars and the public.

Amelia Mary Earhart was born on July 24, 1897, in Atchison, Kansas. From a young age, she displayed a spirit of adventure and independence, traits that would later define her career and public persona. She first became interested in aviation after attending an air show in 1920, where she took a brief flight that solidified her desire to become a pilot. She began taking flying lessons with Neta Snook, one of the few female flight instructors at the time, and quickly proved herself to be a skilled and determined aviator.

In 1928, Earhart gained international fame as the first woman to fly across the Atlantic Ocean, albeit as a passenger. She was part of a three-person crew that flew from Newfoundland to Wales, a journey that garnered significant media attention and cemented her status as a celebrity. However, Earhart was determined to prove herself as a pilot and not just a passenger. In 1932, she made a solo transatlantic flight from Newfoundland to Ireland, becoming the first woman to do so and only the second person after Charles Lindbergh. This achievement earned her numerous accolades, including the Distinguished Flying Cross, and solidified her status as a pioneering figure in aviation.

Earhart continued to set records and push boundaries in aviation, but her most ambitious goal was to become the first person to fly around the world along a route that would follow the equator as closely as possible. This journey would cover approximately 29,000 miles and include stops on five continents. Earhart chose Fred Noonan, a skilled navigator with extensive experience in both marine and aerial navigation, as her co-pilot and navigator for the journey.

The pair departed from Oakland, California, on June 1, 1937, in a twin-engine Lockheed Electra 10E aircraft. Their flight plan took them from Oakland to Miami, where they officially began the world flight. From Miami, they flew to South America, across the Atlantic Ocean to Africa, then eastward across India and Southeast Asia. By June 29, they had reached Lae, New Guinea, having completed about 22,000 miles of the journey.

The next leg of their journey was to take them to Howland Island, a small, uninhabited island in the Pacific Ocean. This leg was particularly challenging because Howland Island is tiny and isolated, making it difficult to locate. The flight was approximately 2,556 miles long, and successful navigation to the island required precise calculations and communication.

On July 2, 1937, Earhart and Noonan took off from Lae, bound for Howland Island. The U.S. Coast Guard cutter Itasca was stationed near the island to provide radio guidance and to establish communication with Earhart's plane. As the flight progressed, Earhart transmitted several messages indicating that they were encountering difficulties. In her last confirmed transmission, she stated that they were "on the line 157 337," which refers to a navigational line running through their intended destination. However, despite numerous attempts by the Itasca to communicate with Earhart and provide assistance, the aircraft was never seen or heard from again.

The disappearance triggered one of the most extensive and expensive search efforts in history at that time. The U.S. Navy and

Coast Guard scoured thousands of square miles of ocean, focusing on the area around Howland Island, but no trace of Earhart, Noonan, or the aircraft was found. On July 19, 1937, the search was officially called off, and Earhart and Noonan were declared lost at sea.

The mystery of Earhart's disappearance has given rise to numerous theories and speculations. One of the most widely accepted theories is that Earhart and Noonan ran out of fuel while searching for Howland Island and were forced to ditch the aircraft in the ocean, where they perished. This theory is supported by the fact that they were low on fuel, as indicated in Earhart's last transmissions, and by the challenging nature of locating such a small island in the vast Pacific.

Another prominent theory suggests that Earhart and Noonan may have landed on an uninhabited island after failing to find Howland Island. One of the most frequently mentioned islands in this theory is Nikumaroro, formerly known as Gardner Island, which is located about 350 miles southeast of Howland Island. This theory gained traction in part due to reports from the island's settlers in the 1940s, who found aircraft wreckage and other artifacts that some believe could be linked to Earhart. Additionally, bones were discovered on the island in 1940, initially thought to be those of a man but later speculated to possibly belong to Earhart. However, subsequent analysis has been inconclusive.

Another theory posits that Earhart and Noonan were captured by the Japanese military, which had control over many Pacific islands at the time. This theory suggests that they may have inadvertently flown into Japanese-held territory and were taken prisoner, possibly on Saipan. Proponents of this theory cite anecdotal reports from locals and U.S. servicemen, as well as claims that Earhart was executed by the Japanese. However, there is no concrete evidence to support this theory, and it is widely regarded as speculative.

Over the years, the search for answers has continued, with numerous expeditions and investigations aiming to uncover the truth behind Earhart's disappearance. The International Group for Historic Aircraft Recovery (TIGHAR) has been particularly active in searching for evidence on Nikumaroro, conducting multiple expeditions to the island and uncovering artifacts that some believe could be linked to Earhart. These include pieces of metal, remnants of a shoe, and a cosmetic jar. However, none of these findings have definitively proven a connection to Earhart.

In 2018, a new forensic analysis of the bones found on Nikumaroro suggested that they could indeed belong to Earhart, challenging earlier assessments. This analysis compared the measurements of the bones to Earhart's known measurements and concluded that the remains were more likely to belong to her than to a man. However, without more conclusive DNA evidence, this theory remains unproven.

The mystery of Amelia Earhart's disappearance endures not only because of the intrigue surrounding her final flight but also because of her legacy as a pioneering aviator and symbol of female empowerment. Earhart broke numerous records and shattered gender barriers in aviation, becoming a role model for women around the world. Her disappearance has only added to her legend, making her an enduring figure in American history and culture.

The story of Amelia Earhart continues to inspire new generations of aviators, explorers, and scholars. Her determination, courage, and adventurous spirit resonate with those who strive to push the boundaries of what is possible. The search for answers about her fate also reflects broader human questions about exploration, risk, and the pursuit of knowledge.

In the end, the disappearance of Amelia Earhart remains an unsolved mystery, one that is likely to continue sparking debate and investigation for years to come. The case embodies the complexities and challenges of early aviation, the dangers of exploration, and the enduring fascination with the unknown. Whether Earhart's final resting place will ever be discovered or whether the full story of her last flight will be revealed, her legacy as a trailblazer and icon endures, a testament to the enduring power of human curiosity and the quest for adventure.

Chapter 6: The Unresolved Case of Jack the Ripper

The unresolved case of Jack the Ripper is one of the most infamous and enduring mysteries in criminal history. This unidentified serial killer, who operated in the impoverished areas of London, particularly the Whitechapel district, in the late 19th century, has become a symbol of the dark underbelly of Victorian society. The murders attributed to Jack the Ripper were characterized by their brutal nature and the killer's apparent surgical precision. Despite numerous investigations and a wealth of theories, the identity of Jack the Ripper remains unknown, and the case continues to intrigue criminologists, historians, and the public alike.

The story of Jack the Ripper begins in the late summer and autumn of 1888, during what came to be known as the "Autumn of Terror." The Ripper is generally believed to have killed at least five women, all of whom were prostitutes, although some researchers argue that the number of victims could be higher. The five canonical victims, as they are known, were Mary Ann Nichols, Annie Chapman, Elizabeth Stride, Catherine Eddowes, and Mary Jane Kelly. These women were killed in a manner that suggested the perpetrator had some anatomical knowledge, leading to speculation that he might have been a surgeon or butcher.

The first canonical victim, Mary Ann Nichols, was discovered on August 31, 1888, in Buck's Row (now Durward Street) in Whitechapel. Her throat had been slashed, and her abdomen was mutilated. This initial murder set a pattern that would be seen in subsequent killings: the use of a knife to inflict deep, lethal wounds, particularly to the throat, and the mutilation of the body, especially the abdomen. The brutality of the crime shocked the public and attracted widespread media attention.

Annie Chapman was the second canonical victim, found on September 8, 1888, in the backyard of 29 Hanbury Street, Spitalfields. Like Nichols, Chapman's throat had been cut, and her abdomen was severely mutilated. In Chapman's case, parts of her internal organs had been removed, a detail that contributed to the belief that the killer possessed some knowledge of anatomy. The removal of organs also suggested a possible ritualistic element to the murders, which has fueled various theories about the killer's motives and identity.

The third and fourth canonical victims, Elizabeth Stride and Catherine Eddowes, were killed on the same night, September 30, 1888, in what is known as the "double event." Stride's body was found in Dutfield's Yard off Berner Street (now Henriques Street). Unlike the other victims, Stride's body was not mutilated, leading to speculation that the killer may have been interrupted. Less than an hour later, Eddowes' mutilated body was found in Mitre Square in the City of London. Her throat had been cut, and her abdomen mutilated, with the removal of some internal organs.

The final canonical victim, Mary Jane Kelly, was murdered on November 9, 1888. Her body was found in her room at 13 Miller's Court, Dorset Street, Spitalfields. Kelly's murder was the most gruesome of all, with her body extensively mutilated and disemboweled. The sheer brutality of the crime, combined with the fact that it occurred indoors, added to the fear and mystery surrounding the case.

The nature of the killings, particularly the mutilations, led to widespread speculation about the identity and motives of the killer. The press played a significant role in shaping public perception of the case, coining the moniker "Jack the Ripper" after a letter purportedly written by the killer was sent to the Central News Agency and widely published. This "Dear Boss" letter, dated September 25, 1888, was signed "Jack the Ripper" and contained threats of further violence.

Although the authenticity of the letter has been questioned, the name stuck and has since become synonymous with the case.

Another infamous piece of correspondence associated with the case is the "From Hell" letter, received by George Lusk, the head of the Whitechapel Vigilance Committee, on October 16, 1888. This letter was accompanied by a small box containing a piece of a human kidney, which the writer claimed belonged to Catherine Eddowes. The letter's crude handwriting and the gory nature of its contents intensified the public's fear and fascination with the killer. However, like the "Dear Boss" letter, the authenticity of the "From Hell" letter is disputed, with some historians suggesting it might have been a hoax.

The police investigation into the Ripper murders was extensive and involved multiple law enforcement agencies, including the Metropolitan Police, the City of London Police, and Scotland Yard. Numerous suspects were considered, and hundreds of interviews were conducted. However, the police were hampered by a lack of forensic technology and the difficulties of conducting a complex investigation in a densely populated urban area. The case files, known as the "Whitechapel Murders," contain records of police efforts, including surveillance, interviews, and the examination of physical evidence, but they ultimately failed to identify the killer.

One of the most enduring aspects of the Jack the Ripper case is the sheer number of suspects who have been proposed over the years. Some of the most notable suspects include Montague John Druitt, a barrister and teacher whose body was found in the Thames shortly after the last canonical murder; Aaron Kosminski, a Polish-Jewish immigrant who was committed to an asylum; Michael Ostrog, a Russian doctor and criminal; and George Chapman, a Polish barber who was later convicted of poisoning several women. Each of these suspects has had proponents who believe they were the Ripper, but none of the theories has been conclusively proven.

The case has also been fertile ground for conspiracy theories and more outlandish suspects. One such theory involves Prince Albert Victor, Duke of Clarence and Avondale, a grandson of Queen Victoria, who has been suggested as a suspect in various conspiracy theories. Another theory posits that the Ripper was actually a woman, sometimes referred to as "Jill the Ripper," though this theory has little supporting evidence.

The mystery of Jack the Ripper has had a lasting impact on popular culture, inspiring countless books, films, and television series. The figure of the Ripper, often depicted as a shadowy figure in a top hat and cloak, has become an icon of fear and intrigue. The case has also influenced the field of criminology, particularly in the development of criminal profiling. The Ripper's actions and the investigation have been studied extensively in an effort to understand the psychology and behavior of serial killers.

One of the challenges in studying the Jack the Ripper case is the difficulty of separating fact from fiction. Over the years, the case has become encrusted with myths, legends, and inaccuracies, making it challenging to discern the truth. Some researchers have pointed out that the sensationalism of the press at the time contributed to the mythologizing of the case, as newspapers competed to provide the most lurid and sensational stories to their readers.

Despite the passage of more than a century, the case of Jack the Ripper remains an open question. Advances in forensic science, particularly DNA analysis, have raised hopes that new evidence might come to light. For example, in recent years, some researchers have attempted to analyze DNA from items purportedly connected to the case, such as a shawl said to have been found near Catherine Eddowes' body. However, the results have been inconclusive, and questions about the chain of custody and contamination of the evidence persist.

The enduring fascination with Jack the Ripper can be attributed to several factors. The gruesome nature of the crimes, the mystery surrounding the killer's identity, and the vivid image of Victorian London's East End as a place of darkness and danger all contribute to the case's lasting appeal. The Ripper's ability to elude capture, despite the efforts of law enforcement and the intense public scrutiny, adds an element of intrigue and frustration to the story.

In the end, the unresolved case of Jack the Ripper serves as a reminder of the limitations of criminal investigations, particularly in the face of an elusive and cunning perpetrator. It also highlights the societal and cultural factors that shape our understanding of crime and justice. The Ripper's victims, who were marginalized and vulnerable women, are often overshadowed in discussions of the case, which tend to focus on the mystery of the killer's identity. Remembering the humanity of the victims and the brutal reality of their murders is an essential part of understanding the impact and legacy of the case.

The case of Jack the Ripper remains one of the most famous unsolved mysteries in history, a haunting reminder of the darkness that can lurk in the shadows of even the most civilized societies. As new generations continue to study and explore the case, the legend of Jack the Ripper will undoubtedly endure, a chilling testament to the enduring power of mystery and the human fascination with the unknown.

Chapter 7: The Lost Colony of Roanoke

The story of the Lost Colony of Roanoke is one of the oldest and most enduring mysteries in American history. It revolves around the first English attempt to establish a permanent settlement in the New World, which mysteriously disappeared without a trace. The events surrounding the Roanoke Colony have fascinated historians, archaeologists, and the public for centuries, spawning numerous theories and speculations about the fate of its inhabitants. The saga is set against the backdrop of Elizabethan England's early efforts at overseas colonization, a period marked by ambition, rivalry, and the harsh realities of life in an unknown land.

The Roanoke Colony was an early English settlement established on Roanoke Island, located in present-day North Carolina. The island was part of the land granted to Sir Walter Raleigh by Queen Elizabeth I, who hoped to expand English influence and establish a foothold in the Americas to rival the Spanish. Raleigh, a prominent courtier and explorer, never personally visited Roanoke but was instrumental in organizing and financing the expeditions. The colony was intended to serve as a base for privateering, a legal form of piracy against Spanish ships, as well as a potential site for a new English society.

The first attempt to establish a colony on Roanoke Island occurred in 1585, led by Sir Richard Grenville and Ralph Lane. This expedition, consisting of 600 men, faced numerous challenges from the outset. They arrived late in the season, which limited their ability to plant crops and secure adequate food supplies. Relations with the local Indigenous peoples, including the Algonquian-speaking tribes, were initially cooperative but soon deteriorated due to cultural misunderstandings and mutual distrust. The colonists' aggressive demands for food and resources, coupled with their suspicion of the Native Americans, led to increasing tensions and violence. By the time English explorer Sir Francis Drake visited the colony in June 1586, the situation had become untenable, and many of the settlers chose to return to England with him.

A second attempt to establish a colony was made in 1587, led by John White, an artist and friend of Raleigh who had accompanied the previous expedition. This group included 115 settlers, men, women, and children, who aimed to create a self-sustaining community rather than a mere military outpost. Among the colonists was White's daughter, Eleanor Dare, who gave birth to Virginia Dare, the first English child born in the New World, shortly after their arrival. The colony faced immediate challenges, including a shortage of supplies and strained relations with the local Native American tribes, who were wary after their previous encounters with the English.

One of the key issues was that the settlers arrived too late in the season to plant crops, leaving them dependent on local resources and supplies from England. As tensions with the Native Americans grew, the colonists found themselves increasingly isolated and vulnerable. In the face of these difficulties, the colony's leaders decided to send Governor White back to England to secure additional supplies and reinforcements. White reluctantly agreed, leaving behind his family and the settlers with the promise to return as quickly as possible.

White's return to England was ill-timed. The Anglo-Spanish War was escalating, and the threat of the Spanish Armada loomed large, diverting England's resources and attention. Queen Elizabeth I ordered that all available ships be kept in England to defend against the anticipated invasion, delaying White's return voyage to Roanoke. It wasn't until 1590, three years after he had left, that White was able to secure passage back to the colony, traveling aboard a privateer fleet.

When White and his party finally arrived at Roanoke Island on August 18, 1590, they found the settlement deserted. There was no sign of the settlers, and the buildings and fortifications had been dismantled. The only clue to the colonists' fate was the word "CROATOAN" carved into a post of the fort and the letters "CRO" carved into a nearby tree. There was no sign of a struggle or distress, and the colonists had left behind no messages indicating where they had gone or what had happened.

The word "Croatoan" referred to both a nearby island, now known as Hatteras Island, and a group of Indigenous people who lived there. The colonists had established friendly relations with the Croatoan tribe during the earlier expeditions, and it was possible that they had sought refuge with them. However, bad weather and the lateness of the season prevented White and his men from conducting a thorough search of the surrounding area, including Croatoan Island. Forced to return to England due to dwindling supplies and the threat of further storms, White left Roanoke without any definitive answers about the fate of the settlers, including his own family.

The disappearance of the Roanoke colonists has remained an enduring mystery, with numerous theories proposed over the centuries. One of the most plausible explanations is that the settlers integrated with local Indigenous tribes, such as the Croatoan or other neighboring groups. This theory suggests that the colonists, facing starvation and isolation, sought help from the Native Americans and gradually assimilated into their communities. Some historians and archaeologists have pointed to accounts from later English explorers and settlers who encountered Native Americans with European features or who spoke English. Additionally, some Native American oral traditions reference the presence of white settlers joining their communities.

Another theory posits that the colonists attempted to relocate inland, possibly towards the Chesapeake Bay area, where they had originally intended to settle before choosing Roanoke. This theory is supported by the fact that the colony's initial instructions included a plan to move further inland if necessary. However, there is little concrete evidence to support this theory, and no remains or artifacts definitively linked to the Roanoke colonists have been found in the Chesapeake area.

Some researchers have speculated that the colonists met a more tragic end, such as falling victim to hostile Indigenous tribes or Spanish forces. The Spanish, who were wary of English encroachment in the New World, had a military presence in the region and were known to have attacked other English settlements. However, there is no direct evidence to suggest that the Spanish were involved in the disappearance of the Roanoke settlers.

Over the years, various archaeological efforts have sought to uncover clues about the fate of the Lost Colony. Excavations on Roanoke Island and surrounding areas have uncovered artifacts from the period, but none have conclusively resolved the mystery. One intriguing find was a series of "dare stones" discovered in the 1930s, which purportedly contained messages from Eleanor Dare and other colonists. The stones' authenticity has been widely debated, with many scholars considering them to be a hoax.

In recent years, advances in technology and new archaeological discoveries have renewed interest in the case. In 2012, researchers examining a 16th-century map drawn by John White discovered a hidden symbol beneath a patch, indicating the possible location of a fort or settlement at the confluence of the Roanoke and Chowan Rivers. This area, known as Site X, has yielded artifacts that suggest a prolonged presence of European settlers, but it remains uncertain whether these artifacts are directly connected to the Lost Colony.

The mystery of the Lost Colony of Roanoke continues to captivate the public imagination, symbolizing the challenges and uncertainties of early European colonization in the New World. The story is a poignant reminder of the difficulties faced by those early settlers, who ventured into an unknown and often hostile environment in search of a new life. The fate of the Roanoke colonists remains a subject of speculation and intrigue, representing both a historical puzzle and a cautionary tale about the perils of colonization.

As historians and archaeologists continue to investigate, the case of the Lost Colony offers insights into the cultural and historical context of the period, including the interactions between European settlers and Indigenous peoples. The mystery also highlights the limitations of historical records and the challenges of reconstructing the past from fragmentary evidence. Whether the fate of the Roanoke colonists will ever be definitively resolved remains uncertain, but their story endures as one of the most enigmatic and enduring chapters in American history.

Chapter 8: The Baffling Yuba County Five

The case of the Yuba County Five, often referred to as the "American Dyatlov Pass" due to its mysterious and tragic nature, involves the unexplained disappearance and deaths of five young men from Yuba City, California, in 1978. The story is marked by a series of baffling events and puzzling discoveries that have left investigators and the public grasping for answers. The men, who were all friends and part of a basketball team for individuals with intellectual disabilities, became the central figures in one of the most perplexing mysteries in modern American history.

The five men involved in the case were Gary Mathias, age 25; Jack Madruga, age 30; Bill Sterling, age 29; Jack Huett, age 24; and Ted Weiher, age 32. Each of these men had varying degrees of intellectual disabilities or psychiatric conditions, but they were generally high-functioning and able to take care of themselves. They shared a passion for sports, particularly basketball, and were eagerly anticipating an upcoming tournament organized by the Special Olympics.

On the evening of February 24, 1978, the group drove to Chico, California, about 50 miles north of Yuba City, to watch a college basketball game. They were last seen purchasing snacks at a convenience store in Chico around 10 p.m., with plans to return home that night. The men were expected to participate in their own basketball game the following day, which they were all excited about. However, they never returned home, and their disappearance set off a widespread search and a series of bizarre and tragic discoveries.

The first significant development in the case came on February 28, 1978, when a forest ranger found the group's car, a 1969 Mercury Montego, abandoned on a remote mountain road near Oroville, in the Plumas National Forest, about 70 miles away from Chico. The car was stuck in a snowdrift, but it was in good condition and had a quarter tank of gas. There was no sign of the men, and the car keys were missing. Strangely, the car was found with the windows rolled down, despite the cold weather, and the car appeared to have been driven through challenging terrain that the owner, Jack Madruga, was unlikely to attempt willingly. Additionally, although the men were not dressed for the cold weather, there were snacks and soda in the car, suggesting they had not been in a hurry when they left Chico.

The search for the missing men intensified, but the harsh winter conditions and difficult terrain hampered efforts. Theories about the group's fate ranged from a planned disappearance to an accident or foul play. Some speculated that the men had become disoriented or lost, while others suggested that they might have encountered someone or something that led to their disappearance.

The mystery deepened on June 4, 1978, when the skeletal remains of Ted Weiher were discovered in a trailer maintained by the U.S. Forest Service, about 19.4 miles from where the car was found. Weiher's body was lying on a bed, wrapped in eight sheets, and had lost nearly half of its weight, suggesting that he had survived for an extended period after the group went missing. Disturbingly, despite the freezing conditions, Weiher had not made use of the ample supplies in the trailer, including canned food, clothing, and matches. The autopsy indicated that he had died of starvation and hypothermia.

Further investigation revealed even more perplexing details. The trailer's propane tank, which could have provided heat, had not been used, and Weiher's feet were frostbitten, though shoes that fit him were found in the trailer. Additionally, Weiher's body showed signs that he had been suffering from gangrene due to his untreated injuries. The discovery of Weiher's body raised more questions than answers: why had he not used the available resources, and what had happened to the other men?

Shortly after Weiher's body was found, searchers discovered the remains of Jack Madruga and Bill Sterling along the road leading to the trailer, at different points but relatively close to each other. Both men had apparently died of hypothermia. Madruga was found clutching his watch, and Sterling's body had been partially consumed by animals. The locations of the bodies suggested that they had tried to reach the trailer or find help but had succumbed to the elements.

The remains of Jack Huett were discovered a few days later, two miles from the trailer, in a heavily wooded area. His bones were scattered, likely by animals, and only a small portion of his body was recovered. The discovery of these four bodies still left one member of the group unaccounted for: Gary Mathias. Unlike the others, Mathias had a history of schizophrenia and required medication to manage his condition. His shoes were found inside the trailer, suggesting that he had survived for a time after Weiher's death and had possibly ventured outside. However, despite extensive searches, Mathias's body was never found, and his fate remains unknown.

The case of the Yuba County Five remains shrouded in mystery, with several key questions unanswered. Why did the men, who were not dressed for cold weather, drive so far off their expected route and into the mountains? The road to the trailer was steep and rough, making it unlikely that they drove there accidentally. If they were seeking help or shelter, why didn't they use the resources in the trailer, which could have saved their lives? And what happened to Gary Mathias, whose body was never recovered?

Numerous theories have been proposed to explain these questions. One theory suggests that the men might have been coerced or forced to drive to the remote area, possibly by someone they encountered on their way home. This theory is supported by the fact that the men were known to be cautious and unlikely to take risks, particularly driving into an unfamiliar and challenging area at night. However, there is no concrete evidence to support the involvement of a third party.

Another theory posits that the group may have experienced a form of shared psychological distress or panic, possibly exacerbated by Gary Mathias's schizophrenia. This could have led them to make irrational decisions, such as abandoning their car and walking into the wilderness. Mathias's mental health condition and the lack of his medication might have played a role in the group's actions, particularly if he became agitated or paranoid.

There is also the possibility that the group simply became lost or disoriented, particularly in the dark and cold conditions. They may have initially left the car to seek help, not realizing the dangers of the terrain and weather. The fact that they did not use the resources in the trailer could suggest that they were disoriented or that they did not fully understand their situation's severity. However, this theory does not fully explain the seemingly purposeful route taken to the remote area or the failure to use available supplies.

The lack of evidence and the contradictory nature of the findings have left the case open to speculation and debate. The families of the men have expressed frustration with the investigation, feeling that not enough was done to explore all possible leads and that the case was closed prematurely. They have also raised concerns about the initial response to the disappearance, which they believe was not taken seriously enough by authorities.

In the years since the incident, the case of the Yuba County Five has become a subject of fascination and speculation. It has been the focus of documentaries, articles, and books, and continues to intrigue those interested in unsolved mysteries and true crime. The case's parallels with the Dyatlov Pass incident, where nine Russian hikers died under mysterious circumstances in the Ural Mountains in 1959, have only added to its mystique.

Despite the passage of time, the case remains unsolved, and the mystery of what happened to the Yuba County Five endures. It is a haunting reminder of how a seemingly ordinary trip can turn into a tragedy under inexplicable circumstances. The fate of the men, particularly Gary Mathias, who remains missing, is a poignant and troubling chapter in the history of unexplained disappearances. The Yuba County Five case challenges our understanding of human behavior and survival and serves as a testament to the enduring nature of unsolved mysteries.

Chapter 9: The Bermuda Triangle Mysteries

The Bermuda Triangle, also known as the Devil's Triangle, is a loosely defined region in the western part of the North Atlantic Ocean where numerous aircraft and ships have disappeared under mysterious circumstances. The triangle's boundaries are generally considered to extend from Miami, Florida, to Bermuda, and then to San Juan, Puerto Rico, before returning to Miami. Covering an area of approximately 500,000 square miles, this enigmatic region has become synonymous with unexplained phenomena, prompting widespread speculation and debate among scientists, historians, and the general public.

The Bermuda Triangle gained significant public attention in the mid-20th century, particularly after a series of high-profile disappearances. One of the earliest and most famous incidents occurred in December 1945, when Flight 19, a squadron of five U.S. Navy Avenger torpedo bombers, vanished during a training mission. Despite extensive search efforts, neither the aircraft nor their 14 crew members were ever found. This incident, along with the disappearance of a rescue plane sent to find them, sparked widespread intrigue and speculation, laying the groundwork for the Bermuda Triangle's modern mythos.

The legend of the Bermuda Triangle, however, predates Flight 19. Reports of strange occurrences in the area date back centuries, with Christopher Columbus reportedly encountering unusual compass readings and a great flame of fire falling into the sea during his voyage in 1492. Sailors and explorers in subsequent centuries reported similar experiences, describing mysterious lights, sudden storms, and other inexplicable phenomena. These accounts contributed to the growing lore surrounding the region, even though many of them could be attributed to the natural challenges of navigating the open ocean.

In the 20th century, the Bermuda Triangle's reputation as a place of mystery and danger was solidified by a series of disappearances involving both aircraft and ships. The USS Cyclops, a U.S. Navy cargo ship, disappeared in 1918 while en route from Barbados to Baltimore, Maryland, with 309 crew members aboard. It remains one of the largest non-combat losses of life in U.S. naval history, and no trace of the ship was ever found. Similar disappearances, including those of the SS Marine Sulphur Queen in 1963 and the cargo ship SS Sandra in 1950, further fueled the legend.

The public's fascination with the Bermuda Triangle was further stoked by popular culture. Books such as Charles Berlitz's "The Bermuda Triangle" (1974) and Richard Winer's "The Devil's Triangle" (1974) popularized theories suggesting that the region was a hub of paranormal activity. These works speculated on various explanations for the disappearances, including extraterrestrial abductions, interdimensional portals, and underwater cities such as Atlantis. The Bermuda Triangle also became a staple of television documentaries, movies, and fictional stories, which often portrayed it as a place of unexplainable and sinister forces.

Despite the sensationalist nature of these accounts, the mystery of the Bermuda Triangle has also attracted serious scientific inquiry. Researchers have proposed a variety of natural explanations for the region's notoriety. One of the most widely accepted theories involves the role of environmental factors, such as unpredictable weather patterns, ocean currents, and magnetic anomalies. The Gulf Stream, a powerful ocean current flowing through the Bermuda Triangle, can cause rapid changes in weather and sea conditions, making navigation challenging and potentially dangerous. Sudden storms, waterspouts, and rogue waves—extremely large and unpredictable waves—are not uncommon in this region and could easily capsize ships or down aircraft.

Magnetic anomalies have also been cited as a potential factor. The Bermuda Triangle is one of the few places on Earth where true north and magnetic north line up, which can cause compass readings to fluctuate and confuse navigators. This phenomenon, known as "magnetic declination," could lead to navigational errors, especially in the days before modern GPS technology. However, this explanation does not account for the fact that similar magnetic anomalies are found in other parts of the world without a corresponding spike in mysterious disappearances.

Another scientific theory involves methane hydrates—crystalline structures containing methane gas trapped beneath the ocean floor. It's hypothesized that sudden releases of methane gas could reduce the density of the water, causing ships to lose buoyancy and sink rapidly. Such gas eruptions could also interfere with aircraft engines, leading to crashes. While this theory is plausible, there is little concrete evidence linking methane hydrates to the specific incidents in the Bermuda Triangle.

Human error is another significant factor in many of the incidents attributed to the Bermuda Triangle. Navigational mistakes, mechanical failures, and inexperienced crews have been cited in numerous cases. The vast area covered by the Bermuda Triangle sees heavy maritime and air traffic, increasing the likelihood of accidents. Moreover, the region's tropical climate is prone to sudden storms and hurricanes, which can contribute to catastrophic events.

Skeptics argue that the Bermuda Triangle's reputation as a site of unusual disappearances is largely a product of myth-making and sensationalism. They point out that the number of incidents in the Bermuda Triangle is not significantly higher, proportionally, than in any other heavily traveled region of the world. Lloyd's of London and the U.S. Coast Guard, two authoritative sources on maritime safety, have stated that the Bermuda Triangle does not have an unusually high incidence of shipwrecks or air accidents. They attribute the legend to a combination of human error, natural environmental factors, and media exaggeration.

Investigations into specific incidents have often revealed more mundane explanations. For instance, the disappearance of Flight 19 is now generally attributed to navigational errors compounded by deteriorating weather conditions, leading to the aircraft running out of fuel and crashing into the sea. Similarly, the loss of the USS Cyclops is believed to have been caused by a combination of structural failure and rough seas, although the exact cause remains unknown due to the lack of wreckage.

Despite these rational explanations, the Bermuda Triangle continues to captivate the imagination of the public and researchers alike. The enduring allure of the Bermuda Triangle lies in the human fascination with the unknown and the unexplained. The combination of unexplained disappearances, the vast and often treacherous ocean environment, and the region's association with navigational anomalies creates a perfect storm of mystery and intrigue. The Bermuda Triangle serves as a canvas onto which people project their fears, fantasies, and theories about the unknown, from alien abductions to lost civilizations.

In recent years, advances in technology have offered new tools for investigating the mysteries of the Bermuda Triangle. Satellite imagery, improved underwater exploration equipment, and advanced navigation systems have provided more detailed data about the region's environment and conditions. These tools have helped to clarify the circumstances surrounding some incidents while debunking myths perpetuated by earlier, less accurate reports. For example, sonar and deep-sea exploration have identified many previously unknown shipwrecks, shedding light on past maritime disasters and helping to distinguish between genuine mysteries and cases that can be explained by known factors.

The Bermuda Triangle also serves as a valuable case study for understanding how myths and legends develop. It highlights the role of storytelling, media influence, and cultural perceptions in shaping public understanding of natural phenomena. The Bermuda Triangle's legend has been reinforced and perpetuated by books, films, and documentaries that emphasize its mysterious aspects, often at the expense of more mundane explanations. This phenomenon is not unique to the Bermuda Triangle but is seen in other areas of popular culture and folklore, where complex or ambiguous situations are simplified into compelling narratives.

Chapter 10: The Tamam Shud Case

The Tamam Shud case, also known as the Mystery of the Somerton Man, is one of Australia's most perplexing and enduring mysteries. On December 1, 1948, the body of an unidentified man was discovered on Somerton Beach near Adelaide, South Australia. The case derives its name from a scrap of paper found hidden in a secret pocket of the man's trousers, which had the words "Tamam Shud" printed on it. These words are Persian, translating to "ended" or "finished," and were torn from the final page of a rare New Zealand edition of "The Rubaiyat of Omar Khayyam," a collection of poems by the 12th-century poet Omar Khayyam.

The man was found lying in a relaxed position against a seawall, dressed in a suit and tie despite the warm weather. Initial observations suggested he had died while sleeping, as there were no signs of violence or a struggle. His pockets contained an unused train ticket from Adelaide to Henley Beach, a bus ticket from the city that could not be traced, a narrow aluminum comb, a half-empty packet of Juicy Fruit chewing gum, an Army Club cigarette packet containing seven cigarettes of a different brand, and a quarter-full box of Bryant & May matches. Interestingly, all identifying labels had been removed from his clothing, and he carried no identification, making it incredibly difficult for authorities to ascertain his identity.

A thorough post-mortem examination revealed no obvious cause of death. The coroner, Thomas Erskine Cleland, noted that the man's spleen was strikingly large and firm, about three times normal size, and his liver was congested with blood. While poisoning was suspected, tests for common toxins returned negative results. The coroner surmised that a fast-acting poison, which left no trace, could have been responsible. Despite these findings, the precise cause of death remained undetermined.

The investigation took a curious turn when a small piece of rolled-up paper was discovered hidden in a fob pocket of the man's trousers during a re-examination of his belongings. The paper bore the words "Tamam Shud." A public appeal led to the discovery of the book from which the scrap had been torn. The book was found in the back seat of an unlocked car near the scene, and the final page from which the words were torn matched exactly. The front and back covers of the book had faint indentations of what appeared to be a local phone number, a second phone number in another state, and a string of letters thought to be a code.

The local phone number was traced to a woman named Jessica Thomson (known as Jestyn), who lived near Somerton Beach. When questioned, Jessica claimed no knowledge of the deceased man or why her number was in his book. She did, however, exhibit visible distress when shown a plaster cast of the man's face, leading some to speculate that she knew more than she was willing to disclose. Her son, Robin, born in 1947, bore a striking resemblance to the deceased, particularly in the shape of his ears and dental structure. This led to speculation that Robin might have been the child of the Somerton Man, although this has never been conclusively proven.

The cryptic letters found in the book were subjected to extensive analysis by both amateur and professional codebreakers, including the Australian Navy. Despite numerous efforts, the code has never been deciphered and remains one of the most tantalizing aspects of the case. Various theories have been proposed about the nature of the code, ranging from it being a simple cipher or acrostic to the possibility of it being a complex military code.

Over the years, numerous hypotheses have emerged regarding the identity and background of the Somerton Man. One prominent theory suggests that he was a spy, given the timing of his death during the Cold War and the cryptic nature of the evidence. His lack of identification, the removal of clothing labels, and the mysterious code all seem to support this notion. Additionally, Adelaide was a significant hub of military and intelligence activity at the time, further fueling speculation.

Another theory posits that the man was involved in a romantic entanglement gone awry, possibly linked to Jessica Thomson. The emotional reaction Jessica displayed when shown the man's bust and her evasive responses during questioning have led some to believe that she may have had a personal connection to him. This theory is further bolstered by the unusual presence of a specific edition of "The Rubaiyat of Omar Khayyam," a book often associated with themes of love and destiny.

Despite extensive investigations and the efforts of countless enthusiasts, the true identity of the Somerton Man and the circumstances leading to his death remain shrouded in mystery. Advances in forensic technology have offered some hope for resolution. In recent years, DNA analysis has become a focal point of the investigation. In 2019, an exhumation of the Somerton Man's body was proposed to extract DNA for genetic testing, aiming to establish his identity through genealogical databases. This approach has had success in other cold cases, but the bureaucratic process and preservation of remains have posed significant challenges.

The Tamam Shud case continues to captivate the public imagination, not only in Australia but globally. It embodies the archetype of an unsolved mystery, complete with elements of intrigue, romance, and espionage. The enduring fascination with this case underscores a collective human desire to seek closure and make sense of the inexplicable. Each new revelation or theory adds another layer to the complex tapestry of the Somerton Man's story, ensuring that the case remains a subject of enduring interest and speculation. As investigative techniques evolve and new technologies emerge, there remains a glimmer of hope that one day the truth behind the Tamam Shud case will be unveiled, providing answers to the questions that have persisted for over seven decades. Until then, the mystery endures, a haunting reminder of the enigmatic nature of human existence and the secrets that sometimes accompany us to the grave.

Chapter 11: The Cryptic Voynich Manuscript

The Voynich Manuscript is an enigmatic and highly mysterious book that has baffled scholars, cryptographers, and linguists for centuries. Named after Wilfrid Voynich, a Polish book dealer who acquired it in 1912, the manuscript consists of approximately 240 pages filled with strange illustrations and text written in an unknown script. The script, referred to as "Voynichese," has never been conclusively deciphered, and the purpose and origin of the manuscript remain subjects of intense speculation and debate.

The manuscript is written on vellum, a fine-quality parchment made from calfskin, which has been radiocarbon-dated to the early 15th century, between 1404 and 1438. This dating places the creation of the manuscript in the early Renaissance period, a time of significant intellectual and artistic activity in Europe. The text is written from left to right, and the pages feature illustrations that are divided into six distinct sections, each with its own thematic content. These sections include botanical, astronomical, biological, cosmological, pharmaceutical, and recipe components.

The botanical section is the largest and consists of drawings of plants and herbs, many of which are unlike any known species. The illustrations are detailed and colorful, depicting plants with roots, leaves, flowers, and fruits. However, none of the plants can be conclusively identified, leading some researchers to believe that they may be entirely fictional or stylized representations of real plants.

The astronomical section contains diagrams of celestial bodies, including the sun, moon, and stars, as well as zodiac symbols. Some pages feature circular diagrams with radiating lines and text, which appear to represent astronomical or astrological charts. The inclusion of these diagrams suggests that the manuscript may have been intended for use in astronomical or astrological studies, although the precise nature of this use remains unclear.

The biological section is perhaps the most perplexing, featuring drawings of nude women, many of whom are depicted interacting with elaborate plumbing-like structures. These structures appear to be connected by fluid-filled tubes, leading some researchers to speculate that this section may be related to alchemical or medical practices. The women are often shown immersed in pools or bathtubs, and the purpose of these illustrations is one of the most hotly debated aspects of the manuscript.

The cosmological section contains more abstract diagrams, including what appear to be maps or charts of unknown lands or territories. These diagrams are highly complex, featuring interconnected shapes and lines, and are accompanied by lengthy passages of text. The cosmological section's content has led some to propose that the manuscript may be a work of speculative cosmography, detailing an imaginary world or universe.

The pharmaceutical section features drawings of containers, such as jars and vessels, along with depictions of herbs and plant parts. This section is often interpreted as a compendium of medicinal or alchemical recipes, suggesting that the manuscript may have been intended for use by an apothecary or herbalist. The recipes, however, are written in the same undeciphered script as the rest of the manuscript, leaving their content and purpose shrouded in mystery.

The final section of the manuscript consists of continuous text, with each paragraph marked by a star-like symbol. This section, often referred to as the "recipes" section, is the most text-heavy and contains no illustrations. The text is arranged in short paragraphs, and each paragraph begins with a larger, capitalized character. The exact nature of this section is unknown, but it is believed to be a collection of recipes, instructions, or incantations.

Despite extensive analysis by numerous experts, the Voynich Manuscript's text remains undeciphered. Cryptographers have applied a wide range of techniques to the manuscript, including frequency analysis, pattern recognition, and computer algorithms, but none have succeeded in unlocking its secrets. The text does not appear to match any known language, cipher, or code, leading some to speculate that it may be a sophisticated hoax or an elaborate piece of art.

Various theories have been proposed regarding the manuscript's authorship and purpose. Some suggest that it may have been created by an unknown medieval alchemist or herbalist, while others believe it could be the work of a secret society or a religious order. The manuscript's intricate illustrations and undeciphered text have also led to the theory that it may be an elaborate artistic creation, intended to mystify and intrigue its viewers.

One of the most persistent theories is that the manuscript was created by Roger Bacon, a 13th-century English philosopher and Franciscan friar known for his work in alchemy, astronomy, and linguistics. Proponents of this theory argue that Bacon's extensive knowledge and interest in ciphers and secret languages make him a plausible candidate for the manuscript's authorship. However, radiocarbon dating places the manuscript's creation several decades after Bacon's death, casting doubt on this theory.

Another prominent theory is that the manuscript was authored by John Dee, an Elizabethan mathematician, astronomer, and occultist, and his associate Edward Kelley, a self-proclaimed medium and alchemist. Dee and Kelley were known for their interest in cryptography, alchemy, and the esoteric arts, and some researchers believe that the manuscript may be a record of their secret knowledge and experiments. However, there is no concrete evidence linking Dee and Kelley to the manuscript.

In recent years, advances in technology have offered new avenues for exploring the Voynich Manuscript. Multispectral imaging and digital analysis have revealed hidden details in the manuscript's illustrations and text, providing new insights into its creation and content. However, these techniques have yet to yield a definitive translation or explanation of the manuscript's mysterious script.

The Voynich Manuscript continues to capture the imagination of scholars, cryptographers, and enthusiasts around the world. Its undeciphered text and enigmatic illustrations offer a tantalizing glimpse into a world of hidden knowledge and forgotten secrets. As researchers continue to explore new methods and technologies, there remains hope that one day the manuscript's mysteries will be unveiled, shedding light on one of history's most enduring enigmas. Until then, the Voynich Manuscript stands as a testament to the enduring allure of the unknown, a puzzle that challenges our understanding of language, art, and the limits of human knowledge.

Chapter 12: The Ghost Ship Mary Celeste

The story of the Mary Celeste is one of the most enduring maritime mysteries in history, capturing the imagination of generations. The Mary Celeste was an American merchant brigantine discovered adrift and deserted in the Atlantic Ocean on December 4, 1872, by the British brig Dei Gratia. The ship was in seaworthy condition, with her cargo intact, and no clear reason why the crew had abandoned her. The mystery deepened as investigations failed to provide a definitive explanation for the circumstances surrounding the abandonment, leading to numerous theories, both plausible and fantastical.

The Mary Celeste was built in Spencer's Island, Nova Scotia, in 1861 and originally named Amazon. After a series of mishaps, she was sold and renamed Mary Celeste in 1869. The ship was 103 feet long and 282 tons, rigged as a brigantine. On November 7, 1872, she departed from New York City bound for Genoa, Italy, with a cargo of denatured alcohol. The ship was captained by Benjamin Briggs, an experienced and respected mariner. Along with him were his wife, Sarah, their two-year-old daughter, Sophia, and a crew of seven experienced sailors, making a total of ten people on board.

The voyage proceeded without incident until the Mary Celeste was found abandoned approximately 400 miles east of the Azores. When the crew of the Dei Gratia boarded the derelict ship, they found the sails set but in poor condition, some of the rigging damaged, and the ship's single lifeboat missing. The cabin and personal belongings were undisturbed, suggesting that whatever caused the crew to leave, it was not a sudden, violent event. The cargo of alcohol was largely intact, with only a few barrels reportedly empty or damaged. The ship's logbook was last updated on November 25, placing the Mary Celeste near the Azores. There were enough provisions on board to last six months, ruling out starvation as a reason for abandonment.

One of the earliest and most enduring theories was that the crew had mutinied. However, there was no sign of violence, and Captain Briggs was known to be a fair and competent leader. Furthermore, the crew were experienced sailors with no known grievances, making mutiny an unlikely scenario. Another theory suggested piracy, but the ship's valuable cargo and personal possessions of the crew were untouched, which pirates would have likely seized.

Natural phenomena were also considered as possible explanations. A waterspout, a type of tornado occurring over the sea, might have frightened the crew into abandoning ship. However, there was no significant damage consistent with such an event. Similarly, a sudden underwater earthquake or a seismic sea wave, or tsunami, might have caused the crew to panic. Yet, the ship was found in good condition with its cargo secure, suggesting that these events, if they occurred, did not cause catastrophic damage.

One of the more plausible theories involves the cargo of denatured alcohol. Some suggest that the barrels may have leaked, causing vapors to build up in the hold. A spark or flame could have ignited the vapors, causing an explosion or the threat of one, prompting the crew to abandon ship temporarily. This theory is supported by the fact that nine of the 1,701 barrels of alcohol were found to be empty, possibly having leaked. However, there was no visible damage from an explosion, and why the crew did not return to the ship remains a question.

The possibility of foul play cannot be entirely dismissed. Some hypothesized that the crew of the Dei Gratia might have found the Mary Celeste, murdered its occupants, and concocted the abandonment story to claim the salvage rights. However, there was no evidence to support this theory, and the crew of the Dei Gratia were highly regarded and had little motive to engage in such a crime.

Another theory involves the possibility of a severe storm. The Mary Celeste might have encountered heavy weather, causing temporary damage and leading the crew to believe the ship was sinking. They might have taken to the lifeboat, intending to return once the storm abated. However, the ship was found in relatively good condition, with no signs of severe storm damage, making this scenario less likely.

Some theories ventured into the realm of the supernatural, suggesting that the ship was cursed or that its crew was abducted by aliens. These ideas, while popular in fiction and folklore, lack any empirical evidence and are generally considered sensationalist rather than serious explanations.

The mystery of the Mary Celeste persisted through various investigations and court hearings. An Admiralty Court in Gibraltar convened to examine the findings, but no definitive conclusion was reached. The court found no evidence of foul play and awarded salvage rights to the crew of the Dei Gratia, though the award was significantly lower than expected, reflecting the court's lingering suspicions.

In the years that followed, the story of the Mary Celeste was embellished and fictionalized, notably by Arthur Conan Doyle, the creator of Sherlock Holmes, who wrote a short story titled "J. Habakuk Jephson's Statement" in 1884. Doyle's story, although fictional, added to the mystique and legend of the Mary Celeste, influencing public perception and spawning numerous other fictional accounts.

Modern investigations, utilizing contemporary forensic and scientific techniques, have yet to provide a definitive answer. Some researchers have revisited the theory of alcohol fumes, suggesting that an explosion might not have been necessary to cause panic; the mere threat of an explosion could have sufficed. Others have considered the possibility of a rogue wave or seaquake, events that were less understood in the 19th century but are now recognized as significant maritime hazards.

The Mary Celeste remains an enduring enigma, a ghost ship whose story continues to fascinate and perplex. Despite the many theories proposed, the true reason for the crew's disappearance remains unknown. The ship's legacy is a testament to the mysteries of the sea and the human imagination's capacity to ponder the unknown. As new discoveries in marine science and historical research emerge, there may yet be hope that one day the fate of the Mary Celeste and her crew will be conclusively revealed. Until then, the ghost ship sails on in the annals of maritime lore, a symbol of the enduring mystery that the oceans hold.

Chapter 13: The Mystery of the Lady of the Dunes

The mystery of the Lady of the Dunes is one of the most baffling unsolved cases in American history, capturing the imagination of true crime enthusiasts and investigators alike. The case begins on July 26, 1974, when a young girl walking her dog in the dunes of Provincetown, Massachusetts, stumbled upon the decomposed body of a woman. The body was discovered in a remote area of the Race Point Dunes, an isolated and difficult-to-reach part of the Cape Cod National Seashore.

The woman was found lying face down on a beach blanket, with a pair of Wrangler jeans and a blue bandana folded under her head. Her hands had been severed, presumably to prevent identification through fingerprints, and her skull had been crushed with what was likely a military entrenching tool, a type of shovel. Additionally, some of her teeth were missing, though dental work indicated she had extensive and expensive dental care, including crowns, a rare feature at the time that suggested she may have come from a wealthier background. Her body was left unclothed from the waist down, and there were signs of sexual assault.

The lack of identification and the brutal nature of the murder set off an intensive investigation. Authorities estimated that the woman had been dead for about two weeks. The initial examination did not reveal any obvious clues about her identity or the circumstances leading to her death. Despite extensive efforts, including dental record checks and missing person reports, the woman's identity remained elusive. This led to her being referred to as the "Lady of the Dunes."

As the investigation progressed, several leads were pursued, but none yielded definitive answers. One of the key methods used to try to identify the Lady of the Dunes was the release of composite sketches and clay reconstructions of her face. These were distributed widely in the hope that someone would recognize her. Over the years, these reconstructions have been updated and improved with new forensic techniques, but despite these efforts, the Lady of the Dunes has remained unidentified.

One of the more intriguing aspects of the case is the potential connection to the film "Jaws," which was being filmed on Martha's Vineyard, not far from Provincetown, around the time of the murder. In 2015, author Joe Hill, son of Stephen King, proposed a theory that the Lady of the Dunes might have been an extra in the movie. Hill noticed a woman in the film who bore a striking resemblance to the composite sketch of the Lady of the Dunes. She wore a blue bandana and jeans, similar to those found with the body. This theory sparked renewed interest in the case, but despite a flurry of media attention, no concrete evidence linking the woman in the film to the Lady of the Dunes has been found.

Another significant theory that has been explored is the possible connection to known criminals active in the area at the time. One such suspect was Hadden Clark, a convicted serial killer with a history of violence against women. Clark reportedly confessed to the murder of the Lady of the Dunes while in prison, even claiming to have buried her hands separately from her body. However, Clark's history of mental illness and his tendency to confess to crimes he did not commit have led many to doubt the veracity of his claims.

Over the years, various other suspects have been considered, including notorious gangster Whitey Bulger. Bulger was known to have frequented Provincetown around the time of the murder and had a history of brutal violence. Some have speculated that the Lady of the Dunes may have been a victim of Bulger or his associates, but again, no solid evidence has been found to support this theory.

In addition to these theories, advances in forensic science have offered new avenues for investigation. In recent years, DNA testing has been employed in an attempt to identify the Lady of the Dunes.

In 2010, her remains were exhumed to extract DNA samples, which were then entered into national databases. Despite these efforts, no matches have been found. The use of genetic genealogy, a technique that has recently been successful in solving other cold cases, has also been explored, though it has yet to yield any breakthroughs.

The case has also seen a significant amount of public and media attention, with various documentaries, podcasts, and books examining the mystery of the Lady of the Dunes. Each new wave of interest brings fresh tips and theories, though none have provided the definitive answers that investigators and the public seek. The internet, with its vast array of forums and amateur sleuths, has become a hotbed of speculation and analysis, keeping the case in the public eye.

One of the enduring elements of the mystery is the question of why the Lady of the Dunes was killed and who she might have been. Some theories suggest she was a victim of domestic violence, perhaps killed by a jealous lover or spouse. Others propose that she was involved in criminal activities, either as a participant or an unwitting victim. The fact that her hands were severed suggests a level of premeditation and an attempt to conceal her identity, indicating that her killer may have been someone who knew her well.

The psychological profile of the killer has been a subject of much debate. The brutality of the murder, combined with the meticulous effort to hide the victim's identity, suggests a deeply disturbed individual. The use of a military entrenching tool as the murder weapon indicates a certain level of preparedness and strength. The removal of the hands, in particular, points to a calculated attempt to hinder identification, a tactic not commonly seen in most murders.

Despite the passage of time, the determination to solve the case has not waned. The Provincetown Police Department, along with state and federal agencies, continues to investigate leads and explore new technologies that might help identify the Lady of the Dunes and her killer. The case remains open, with law enforcement hopeful that advances in forensic science or a crucial tip from the public might one day bring resolution.

The story of the Lady of the Dunes is a haunting reminder of the many unsolved mysteries that linger in the annals of crime history. It underscores the challenges faced by investigators in identifying victims and solving cases without the modern tools available today. It also highlights the human aspect of such cases – the families and friends who may still be wondering what happened to their loved one.

In the end, the Lady of the Dunes remains a poignant symbol of the unknown, a victim whose identity and story have been lost to time but who continues to inspire a quest for justice. Her case serves as a testament to the relentless pursuit of truth by law enforcement and the enduring fascination with mysteries that defy explanation. Until her identity is uncovered and her killer brought to justice, the Lady of the Dunes will remain an enigmatic figure, haunting the dunes of Provincetown and the imaginations of all who seek to unravel her story.

Chapter 14: The Phantom of Heilbronn

The Phantom of Heilbronn, also known as the Woman Without a Face, was one of Germany's most elusive and confounding criminal figures, responsible for a series of crimes that spanned over a decade. From 1993 to 2009, the Phantom was implicated in more than 40 crimes across Germany, Austria, and France, ranging from petty theft to murder. Despite extensive efforts by law enforcement agencies, the Phantom remained unidentifiable, leaving a trail of DNA evidence but no clear leads. The mystery surrounding the Phantom deepened over the years, leading to widespread speculation and numerous theories about the perpetrator's identity and motives.

The first known crime linked to the Phantom occurred in 1993, when the DNA of an unknown female was found at the scene of a murder in Idar-Oberstein, Germany. A 62-year-old woman had been strangled with a wire, and investigators found DNA on a cup in the victim's kitchen. This DNA would later reappear at various crime scenes, creating a baffling pattern. The Phantom's most notorious crime was the murder of Michèle Kiesewetter, a 22-year-old police officer, in Heilbronn on April 25, 2007. Kiesewetter and her partner were ambushed in their patrol car, and her partner was seriously injured but survived. DNA found on Kiesewetter's service pistol and handcuffs matched the Phantom, bringing the case into the national spotlight.

The crimes attributed to the Phantom were diverse in nature and geographical spread, which made the investigation extraordinarily challenging. The Phantom's DNA was found at the scenes of burglaries, robberies, and even car thefts. Some of the crimes were violent, while others were relatively minor, but the common thread was the presence of the same unknown female DNA. The Phantom's apparent ability to evade capture, despite leaving DNA evidence, perplexed investigators and fueled speculation about her identity. Theories ranged from the possibility of a female serial killer to an accomplice leaving deliberate false trails to mislead the police.

The investigation into the Phantom of Heilbronn involved extensive collaboration between various police departments and forensic experts. Given the widespread nature of the crimes, the case became a high priority, and significant resources were allocated to solve it. Advanced DNA profiling techniques were employed, and numerous individuals were questioned and tested. The crimes attributed to the Phantom spanned diverse locations, including rural areas and urban centers, further complicating the search. Investigators explored the possibility of the Phantom being part of a criminal organization or gang, but no concrete evidence supported this theory.

The turning point in the investigation came in 2009, when the case took an unexpected and dramatic twist. Austrian authorities were investigating the discovery of a charred male body in a burnt-out caravan. DNA from the body and the scene was analyzed, and to the astonishment of the investigators, the Phantom's DNA was found on a small scrap of fabric. The presence of the Phantom's DNA on an object at such an unlikely crime scene raised new questions and doubts. Forensic experts began to reconsider the reliability of the DNA evidence that had been the cornerstone of the investigation for years.

Upon re-evaluation, a startling realization emerged: the DNA evidence was contaminated. The DNA profile of the Phantom had been introduced to the crime scenes through contaminated cotton swabs used for sample collection. The swabs, manufactured by a single company, were found to have been inadvertently contaminated by a female worker during the production process. This revelation was both a breakthrough and a significant setback. It explained why the same DNA had appeared at so many unrelated crime scenes but also meant that the Phantom did not exist as an individual perpetrator. The contamination issue exposed a critical flaw in forensic procedures and underscored the need for stringent quality control measures.

The discovery of the contamination had profound implications for the cases linked to the Phantom. Many investigations had to be reopened, and convictions based on the DNA evidence were called into question. The law enforcement agencies involved faced scrutiny and criticism for the oversight, and the credibility of forensic science was momentarily shaken. The Phantom of Heilbronn case highlighted the complexities and potential pitfalls of relying heavily on DNA evidence without corroborating it with other investigative methods. It served as a cautionary tale for the criminal justice system, emphasizing the importance of rigorous standards and cross-verification in forensic analysis.

In the aftermath of the revelation, efforts were made to prevent similar incidents in the future. Forensic labs implemented more stringent protocols to ensure the integrity of DNA samples, and manufacturers of forensic supplies enhanced their quality control measures. The Phantom of Heilbronn case also sparked broader discussions about the limits and reliability of forensic evidence in criminal investigations. It underscored the need for a holistic approach that combines DNA analysis with traditional detective work, witness statements, and other forms of evidence to build a robust and reliable case.

Despite the resolution of the Phantom mystery, the case left an indelible mark on the field of forensic science and law enforcement. It demonstrated the potential for human error and contamination to mislead investigations and the importance of continually advancing forensic methodologies to safeguard against such issues. The case also reaffirmed the critical role of interdisciplinary collaboration in solving complex crimes and the necessity of maintaining a balance between scientific evidence and other investigative tools.

The story of the Phantom of Heilbronn, from its beginnings as a perplexing series of crimes to its conclusion as a case of contamination, remains a poignant reminder of the challenges and uncertainties inherent in criminal investigations. It serves as a testament to the perseverance of law enforcement agencies and forensic scientists in their quest for truth, as well as the evolving nature of forensic science in addressing and overcoming its own limitations. The Phantom may have been a figment of contaminated evidence, but the lessons learned from the case continue to resonate, shaping the future of forensic investigation and ensuring greater vigilance in the pursuit of justice.

Chapter 15: The Dyatlov Pass Incident

The Dyatlov Pass Incident is one of the most perplexing and enduring mysteries of the 20th century, capturing the imagination and curiosity of investigators, researchers, and the public for over six decades. Named after Igor Dyatlov, the leader of the ill-fated expedition, the incident occurred in the Ural Mountains of the Soviet Union in 1959. A group of nine experienced hikers set out on a trek but met a gruesome and inexplicable fate, their bodies discovered under bizarre and disturbing circumstances. Despite numerous investigations and theories, the true cause of their deaths remains unsolved, shrouded in speculation and intrigue.

On January 23, 1959, a group of ten students and graduates from the Ural Polytechnical Institute in Sverdlovsk (now Yekaterinburg) embarked on a skiing expedition to reach Otorten, a mountain 10 kilometers north of the site where they would eventually meet their end. The team was led by 23-year-old Igor Dyatlov, an experienced hiker and skier. The group consisted of eight men and two women, all seasoned in mountain expeditions. However, one member, Yuri Yudin, fell ill and turned back on January 28, a decision that would ultimately save his life.

The remaining nine hikers continued their journey, documenting their progress with diaries and photographs. On February 1, they reached the eastern slopes of Kholat Syakhl, a name that translates to "Dead Mountain" in the indigenous Mansi language. Due to worsening weather conditions and visibility, they deviated from their planned route and decided to set up camp on the slope rather than moving to a forested area a mile downhill, which would have offered more shelter.

When the group failed to return as scheduled on February 12, concerns were initially muted, as delays in such expeditions were common. However, by February 20, the families of the hikers demanded a rescue operation. The search began with volunteer students and teachers, eventually involving the Soviet Army and police forces. On February 26, rescuers found the group's abandoned and badly damaged tent on Kholat Syakhl. The tent was oddly cut open from the inside, and all the hikers' belongings, including shoes and warm clothes, were left behind, suggesting a hasty and urgent escape.

Footprints of eight or nine people, wearing only socks or a single shoe or even barefoot, were found leading down the slope toward the edge of a nearby forest, about 1.5 kilometers northeast of the campsite. At the forest's edge, under a large Siberian pine tree, the searchers discovered the remains of a small fire and the bodies of Yuri Doroshenko and Georgy Krivonischenko, both shoeless and dressed only in underwear. Branches on the tree were broken up to five meters high, suggesting that one of the hikers had climbed up to look for something, possibly the campsite.

As the search continued, more bodies were found between the pine tree and the campsite: Igor Dyatlov, Zinaida Kolmogorova, and Rustem Slobodin, who appeared to have died in poses suggesting they were attempting to return to the tent. The positions of their bodies and the state of undress indicated a desperate and disoriented attempt to survive in the freezing conditions. Slobodin's skull showed a small crack, but it was not deemed a fatal injury.

It wasn't until May 4, over two months later, that the remaining four hikers were found under four meters of snow in a ravine further into the woods. These bodies presented even more puzzling and gruesome injuries. Nikolai Thibeaux-Brignolle had major skull damage, while Lyudmila Dubinina and Semyon Zolotaryov had severe chest fractures, with the force of the injuries compared to a car crash. Dubinina was also missing her tongue, eyes, and part of her lips, and she had extensive facial damage. Strangely, there were no external wounds or signs of struggle.

The official Soviet investigation concluded that the group members had all died of hypothermia, but the case was closed with the ambiguous statement that they had died due to a "compelling natural force." No additional details were provided, and the case files were sealed, further fueling speculation and conspiracy theories. The strange and violent injuries, the state of undress, and the absence of clear evidence of external threats or an avalanche left many questions unanswered.

Over the years, numerous theories have been proposed to explain the Dyatlov Pass Incident. These range from natural disasters to more exotic explanations. One prominent theory is that an avalanche forced the hikers to flee their tent in a panic. However, the slope angle of their campsite was not steep enough for a typical avalanche, and no evidence of an avalanche was found. Another theory suggests a "katabatic wind," a rare and powerful downward wind that can cause sudden drops in temperature and disorientation, which might explain the frantic escape.

Some theories ventured into the realm of the paranormal or extraterrestrial. Speculations about UFOs and alien abductions were fueled by reports of strange lights seen in the sky around the time of the incident. Additionally, there were mentions of high levels of radiation found on some of the clothing, though these claims were inconsistently reported and not corroborated by all sources. The Soviet military was also conducting missile tests in the region at the time, leading to theories of accidental military involvement or cover-ups.

Another compelling theory involves infrasound, a phenomenon where low-frequency sound waves generated by wind interacting with the terrain can induce feelings of panic, fear, and disorientation in humans. This could potentially explain the irrational behavior of the hikers, but it remains speculative as there is no direct evidence linking infrasound to the incident.

The indigenous Mansi people were initially suspected due to the remote location and the translation of Kholat Syakhl as "Dead Mountain." However, there was no evidence of other human presence in the area, and the Mansi were known to be peaceful and cooperative with Soviet authorities. Thus, this theory was quickly dismissed.

In 2019, the Russian authorities reopened the investigation, focusing on three possible natural explanations: an avalanche, a snow slab, and a hurricane. The conclusion reached in 2020 suggested that a combination of a snow slab (a small, localized avalanche) and hypothermia was the likely cause. The theory posited that a sudden snow slab hit the tent, causing panic and injuries, leading the hikers to abandon their camp inadequately dressed and succumb to hypothermia. While this explanation provides a plausible scenario, it still leaves many details unaccounted for, and not all experts agree with this conclusion.

The Dyatlov Pass Incident remains a subject of fascination and speculation, with new theories and interpretations emerging regularly. It has inspired books, documentaries, films, and countless discussions in both academic circles and popular culture. The incident is a reminder of the unforgiving power of nature and the limits of human understanding when faced with incomplete evidence and the mysteries of the wilderness. Despite modern technology and forensic advances, the true cause of the Dyatlov Pass tragedy may never be conclusively determined, ensuring its place as one of history's most enigmatic and haunting tales.

Chapter 16: The Black Dahlia Murder

The Black Dahlia murder is one of the most infamous and enduring unsolved crimes in American history. The case involves the brutal killing of Elizabeth Short, a young aspiring actress whose mutilated body was discovered in Los Angeles on January 15, 1947. The mystery surrounding her death has captivated the public and investigators for decades, spawning numerous books, films, and theories. The case's combination of gruesome details, a lack of solid leads, and a plethora of suspects has ensured its place in the annals of criminal lore.

Elizabeth Short, born on July 29, 1924, in Boston, Massachusetts, grew up in Medford, a suburb of Boston. Her father, Cleo Short, abandoned the family when she was just five years old, leading to a challenging upbringing for Elizabeth and her four sisters. As a teenager, Elizabeth developed a fascination with Hollywood and dreamed of becoming a star. She moved to California in pursuit of her ambitions, living in various cities and struggling to make ends meet while seeking opportunities in the entertainment industry.

Short's nickname, "The Black Dahlia," reportedly came from her penchant for wearing black clothing and a rumored fascination with the film "The Blue Dahlia," a popular movie at the time. Despite her dreams of fame, Elizabeth led a transient and precarious life, moving frequently and relying on friends and acquaintances for support. She was known to frequent nightclubs and bars in Los Angeles, mingling with various people, including those on the fringes of Hollywood society.

On January 15, 1947, Short's body was discovered by a local resident, Betty Bersinger, in a vacant lot in the Leimert Park neighborhood of Los Angeles. The sight was shocking: Elizabeth's body had been severed in half at the waist, drained of blood, and posed with her arms raised above her head and her legs spread apart. Her face had been brutally slashed from the corners of her mouth to her ears, creating a ghastly "Glasgow smile." Additionally, her body bore signs of torture, including numerous cuts and abrasions, suggesting she had endured a prolonged and horrific ordeal before her death.

The discovery of Short's body immediately drew intense media attention. The press dubbed her "The Black Dahlia," and sensationalized reporting ensued, with lurid headlines and speculative stories capturing the public's imagination. The Los Angeles Police Department (LAPD) launched an extensive investigation, led by detectives Harry Hansen and Finis Brown. Despite their efforts, the investigation was hampered by the lack of concrete evidence and the overwhelming number of false leads and confessions that poured in from the public.

Over the years, numerous suspects have been proposed, and the case has generated a multitude of theories, each with varying degrees of plausibility. One of the earliest suspects was Robert "Red" Manley, a married salesman who was one of the last people seen with Short before her death. Manley had driven Elizabeth from San Diego to Los Angeles and dropped her off at the Biltmore Hotel. He was subjected to intense questioning and even a polygraph test, but he was eventually cleared of any involvement in the crime.

Another prominent suspect was George Hodel, a physician whose son, Steve Hodel, a former LAPD detective, has extensively argued for his father's guilt. Steve Hodel's investigation, detailed in his book "Black Dahlia Avenger," presents circumstantial evidence linking George Hodel to the crime, including suspicious photographs and alleged connections to other unsolved murders. George Hodel's questionable activities, including accusations of incest and his subsequent flight to Asia, have fueled speculation, but definitive proof remains elusive.

The case has also seen attention focused on other figures in the Los Angeles underworld, including individuals with connections to organized crime and the city's dark underbelly. Suspects such as Mark

Hansen, a nightclub owner who knew Short, and Leslie Dillon, a bellhop with a fascination for crime, were investigated but ultimately released due to lack of evidence. The case's complexity and the myriads of potential suspects have made it challenging to narrow down the true culprit.

In addition to the suspects, the investigation was plagued by issues of jurisdictional conflicts and corruption within the LAPD. The department's reputation at the time was marred by scandals and allegations of collusion with organized crime, which further complicated the search for Elizabeth Short's killer. Key evidence, such as a purse and shoe believed to belong to Short, was found in a trash bin several miles from the crime scene but yielded no substantial leads.

The Black Dahlia case has continued to intrigue and baffle both amateur sleuths and professional investigators. Over the decades, advancements in forensic science have been applied to the evidence, but no definitive breakthroughs have emerged. The case remains officially unsolved, with many believing that critical information was either lost or overlooked during the initial investigation.

In the realm of popular culture, the Black Dahlia murder has inspired countless works of fiction and non-fiction, from James Ellroy's novel "The Black Dahlia" to numerous documentaries and feature films. The story's blend of Hollywood glamour, brutal violence, and enduring mystery has cemented its place in American crime lore, prompting ongoing interest and speculation.

The enduring fascination with the Black Dahlia case lies not only in the gruesome details of the murder but also in the broader context of post-war Los Angeles. The city's burgeoning film industry, combined with the influx of hopeful young women seeking stardom, created a backdrop of dreams and desperation. Elizabeth Short's tragic fate is often viewed as a symbol of the darker side of the American dream, where the pursuit of fame and fortune can lead to exploitation and danger.

As the decades have passed, the case has periodically resurfaced in the media, each time reigniting public interest and debate. New theories and suspects continue to emerge, with some researchers even suggesting that the Black Dahlia murder could be connected to other unsolved cases from the same era. The lack of closure has ensured that Elizabeth Short's story remains a compelling and haunting chapter in the annals of crime history.

Chapter 17: The Disappearance of the Beaumont Children

The disappearance of the Beaumont children is one of Australia's most haunting and enduring mysteries, a case that has gripped the nation for decades and remains unsolved to this day. On January 26, 1966, three siblings—Jane, aged 9, Arnna, aged 7, and Grant, aged 4—vanished from Glenelg Beach, a popular seaside destination near Adelaide, South Australia. Despite extensive searches, investigations, and numerous theories, the fate of the Beaumont children remains unknown, and the case continues to be a poignant reminder of the vulnerability of children and the devastating impact of such disappearances on families and communities.

The Beaumont children lived with their parents, Jim and Nancy Beaumont, in the Adelaide suburb of Somerton Park. On the morning of their disappearance, a scorching hot Australia Day, the children eagerly set out for Glenelg Beach, a trip they had made several times before. It was common for children in the area to travel independently, and the Beaumont siblings took the bus alone, planning to return by midday. They were last seen around 10:00 AM, happily playing on the beach and later buying snacks at a local bakery.

When the children failed to return home, their worried mother, Nancy, alerted her husband, Jim, who was at work. They began a frantic search, checking with neighbors, friends, and the bus company, but there was no sign of Jane, Arnna, or Grant. By evening, the police were notified, and a massive search operation was launched. Volunteers, police officers, and even the Australian Army joined in, scouring the beach, surrounding areas, and local waterways. Despite these efforts, no trace of the children was found.

Witnesses reported seeing the Beaumont children with a tall, thin man in his mid-30s, with a sun-tanned complexion and blonde hair.

This man was described as friendly and appeared to be familiar with the children, which led to speculation that he might have gained their trust. He was seen playing with them on the beach and later helping them with their belongings. The children's relaxed demeanor suggested they were not initially alarmed by his presence. This crucial lead, however, did not yield any definitive clues.

The disappearance of the Beaumont children generated an unprecedented level of media coverage and public interest. The case shocked the nation and led to widespread fear and anxiety, particularly among parents. For years, the story dominated headlines, and the search for the children became a national obsession. Despite the intense focus and numerous reported sightings and tips, the investigation remained stymied by a lack of concrete evidence and reliable witnesses.

Several suspects emerged over the years, but none were conclusively linked to the disappearance. One of the most prominent suspects was a man named Derek Percy, a convicted child murderer. Percy was known to have been in the area at the time, and his violent history made him a plausible suspect. However, there was insufficient evidence to charge him, and he consistently denied any involvement in the case.

Another suspect was Bevan Spencer von Einem, a convicted murderer and child molester. Von Einem was implicated in the disappearance and murder of other young men in the Adelaide area during the 1980s. Some investigators believed that he might have been involved in the Beaumont case, but again, no definitive evidence could be found to link him to the crime. Von Einem's connections to a possible network of abusers raised further questions, but the investigation did not result in any breakthroughs.

The case also attracted various conspiracy theories, ranging from suggestions of organized crime involvement to claims of high-level cover-ups. One particularly persistent theory involved a connection to the so-called "Family Murders," a series of brutal killings in Adelaide in the 1970s and 1980s. Some theorists speculated that the Beaumont children might have fallen victim to the same group of perpetrators, but these claims remained speculative and unproven.

Over the years, the Beaumont case has seen periodic resurgences in interest, often spurred by new leads or technological advancements. Forensic techniques, such as DNA testing, have been applied to the evidence, but no conclusive results have emerged. Psychics and private investigators have also offered their services, but their contributions have been largely discounted by authorities.

In 2013, a new search was conducted at a factory site in Adelaide, based on a tip from a former detective who believed that the children's remains might be buried there. The search, which involved ground-penetrating radar and excavation, ultimately yielded no significant findings. Similarly, other leads and potential burial sites have been investigated over the years, but each time, hopes were dashed when no new evidence was uncovered.

The impact of the Beaumont children's disappearance on their family has been profound and heartbreaking. Jim and Nancy Beaumont endured decades of uncertainty and grief, always hoping for a resolution but never receiving the closure they desperately sought. Their lives were irrevocably altered by the loss, and the case remained an open wound for them until their deaths. Jim Beaumont passed away in 2019, and Nancy Beaumont, who continued to live in Adelaide, passed away in 2019 as well.

The disappearance also had a lasting effect on the Australian public and law enforcement. It led to changes in police procedures and an increased awareness of child safety. The case underscored the need for better coordination and communication among law enforcement agencies and highlighted the importance of community vigilance in protecting children. Despite these improvements, the Beaumont case remains a stark reminder of the challenges and frustrations inherent in missing persons investigations.

In popular culture, the Beaumont children's disappearance has been the subject of numerous books, documentaries, and articles. The case has inspired fictionalized accounts and has been referenced in various forms of media, reflecting its enduring grip on the public imagination. Each retelling and reexamination of the case serves to keep the memory of Jane, Arnna, and Grant alive and underscores the tragic nature of their disappearance.

In recent years, advancements in technology and forensic science have offered new hope for resolving cold cases, including the Beaumont disappearance. Techniques such as familial DNA testing, which have been successful in solving other long-standing cases, hold the potential to uncover new leads. However, the passage of time and the degradation of evidence present significant challenges. The case remains open, and investigators continue to review any new information that emerges.

The disappearance of the Beaumont children is a case that exemplifies the enduring mystery and profound sorrow of missing persons cases. It is a story of loss and unresolved grief, of a family and a nation searching for answers that remain elusive. As time goes on, the hope of finding a resolution diminishes, but the memory of Jane, Arnna, and Grant Beaumont endures. Their story is a testament to the resilience of those left behind and the unyielding human desire for closure and justice.

Chapter 18: The Death of Natalie Wood

The death of Natalie Wood is one of Hollywood's most enduring and controversial mysteries, involving a combination of glamour, tragedy, and unanswered questions that continue to captivate the public and media. Natalie Wood, a beloved actress known for her roles in classic films such as "West Side Story" and "Rebel Without a Cause," died under mysterious circumstances on November 29, 1981. Her body was found floating in the waters off Catalina Island, California, near the yacht "Splendour," which she had been aboard with her husband, Robert Wagner, and actor Christopher Walken. The circumstances surrounding her death have been the subject of speculation, investigation, and re-investigation for decades.

Natalie Wood was born Natalia Nikolaevna Zakharenko on July 20, 1938, in San Francisco, California, to Russian immigrant parents. She began her acting career as a child, quickly gaining fame and critical acclaim. Wood transitioned successfully into adult roles, earning three Academy Award nominations and becoming one of Hollywood's most sought-after actresses. Her marriage to Robert Wagner, a leading actor of the time, was one of the most high-profile relationships in Hollywood, adding to her public persona as an iconic star.

The events leading up to Natalie Wood's death began on Thanksgiving weekend in 1981. Wood, Wagner, and Walken, her co-star in the film "Brainstorm," decided to spend the weekend on Wagner and Wood's yacht, "Splendour." The yacht was anchored near Catalina Island, a popular and picturesque getaway off the coast of Southern California. The weekend was supposed to be a relaxing escape, but it quickly turned into a tragedy.

According to the official account at the time, the group had dinner at a restaurant on the island on the night of November 28, 1981, and returned to the yacht afterward. The details of what happened next are murky and have been the subject of much debate. It is known that there was drinking involved, and a heated argument allegedly took place between Wagner and Walken. Wagner later admitted to smashing a wine bottle during the argument, but accounts differ as to whether the argument was about Wood's career or personal issues.

Sometime later, it was discovered that Wood was missing, and the yacht's dinghy, "Valiant," was also gone. Wagner initially assumed that Wood had taken the dinghy to shore, possibly due to the argument, but she was not found on the island. A search was launched, and in the early hours of November 29, Wood's body was found floating face down in the water, about a mile away from the yacht. She was dressed in a nightgown, socks, and a down jacket.

The initial autopsy report concluded that Wood had died from accidental drowning, noting the presence of bruises on her body that were consistent with falling into the water. It was theorized that she may have slipped while trying to secure the dinghy, which had been found nearby with its oars locked. Alcohol and medication were found in her system, which might have impaired her judgment and contributed to the accident. The case was officially closed as an accidental drowning, but the public and media were not satisfied with this explanation.

Theories and suspicions surrounding Wood's death began almost immediately. Many questioned the bruises on her body, suggesting they could indicate foul play. There were also inconsistencies in the statements given by Wagner, Walken, and the yacht's captain, Dennis Davern. Davern, in particular, changed his story over the years, adding to the suspicion. Initially, he supported the accidental drowning theory, but later he claimed that Wagner had been involved in Wood's death and that there had been a cover-up.

In 2011, 30 years after her death, the Los Angeles County Sheriff's Department reopened the case, citing new information from Davern and other sources. The investigation brought renewed media attention and scrutiny, with many hoping for new revelations. In 2012, the coroner's office amended Wood's death certificate, changing the cause of death from "accidental drowning" to "drowning and other undetermined factors." The report noted that the bruises on Wood's body were "likely sustained before she entered the water," suggesting that her death might not have been a simple accident.

Despite the reopening of the case and the reclassification of her death, no new charges were filed, and many questions remained unanswered. Wagner, now in his 90s, has consistently denied any wrongdoing and maintains that Wood's death was a tragic accident. Walken has also remained largely silent on the matter, sticking to his initial statements and declining to speculate on the events of that night.

The mystery of Natalie Wood's death has been the subject of numerous books, documentaries, and films. One of the most notable books is "Goodbye Natalie, Goodbye Splendour" by Marti Rulli and Dennis Davern, which presents the captain's revised account of the events and argues for a more sinister explanation. Various documentaries have also explored the case, including those that feature interviews with people close to Wood and experts who analyze the evidence.

Public fascination with the case is fueled by several factors, including Wood's status as a beloved Hollywood star, the involvement of high-profile figures like Wagner and Walken, and the conflicting accounts and theories. The case touches on themes of love, jealousy, and the dark side of celebrity, which continue to resonate with audiences. The enduring mystery also raises broader questions about the nature of justice and the challenges of solving complex cases with limited evidence.

In 2018, the case was again in the spotlight when the Los Angeles County Sheriff's Department named Wagner as a person of interest, citing inconsistencies in his account and new witness statements. Despite this development, no charges were filed, and the investigation remains open. The lack of definitive answers has ensured that the case continues to be a subject of speculation and intrigue.

The impact of Natalie Wood's death on her family has been profound. Wagner, who was deeply in love with Wood, has had to live under the shadow of suspicion for decades. Wood's daughters, Natasha Gregson Wagner and Courtney Wagner, have also had to cope with the loss of their mother and the ongoing public scrutiny of the case. In recent years, Natasha Gregson Wagner has spoken publicly about her mother's legacy and her own efforts to come to terms with the tragedy.

In the broader context of Hollywood history, Natalie Wood's death is a stark reminder of the vulnerability and pressures faced by those in the public eye. Her career, marked by success and acclaim, was tragically cut short, and her death remains a symbol of the dark and sometimes dangerous undercurrents of the entertainment industry. The case continues to serve as a cautionary tale about the potential for tragedy even among the most glamorous and seemingly fortunate individuals.

As the years go by, the chances of finding definitive answers about Natalie Wood's death diminish, but the case remains open, and investigators continue to review new information as it comes to light. The enduring mystery ensures that Wood's story will continue to be told and retold, keeping her memory alive and highlighting the enduring human desire for truth and justice. Natalie Wood's death, shrouded in uncertainty and controversy, remains one of Hollywood's most compelling unsolved mysteries, a case that continues to captivate and intrigue, ensuring that the legacy of this talented actress will endure for generations to come.

Chapter 19: The Disappearance of Madeleine McCann

The disappearance of Madeleine McCann is one of the most widely reported and controversial missing persons cases in modern history, drawing immense media attention and sparking a global search that continues to this day. Madeleine Beth McCann, a British child, went missing from her bed in a holiday apartment in Praia da Luz, a resort in the Algarve region of Portugal, on the evening of May 3, 2007. She was just three years old at the time, and her disappearance has since become a poignant symbol of the vulnerability of children and the anguish of their families when they go missing.

Madeleine was on vacation with her parents, Kate and Gerry McCann, and her younger twin siblings, Sean and Amelie. The McCanns, both doctors, had traveled to Portugal with a group of family friends and their children. The group, known as the "Tapas Seven," stayed in the Ocean Club Resort, where they spent their days enjoying the beach and the pool, and their evenings dining at the resort's tapas restaurant.

On the night of Madeleine's disappearance, her parents had left her and the twins asleep in their ground-floor apartment while they dined with their friends at a restaurant located about 55 meters away. The adults took turns checking on the children at regular intervals. When Kate McCann checked at around 10:00 PM, she discovered that Madeleine was missing and raised the alarm. What followed was a frantic search by the resort staff, local police, and residents, but there was no sign of Madeleine.

The initial investigation by the Portuguese police, the Polícia Judiciária (PJ), was heavily criticized for its perceived mishandling of the case. Key areas were not sealed off, potential evidence was not adequately preserved, and leads were not pursued with the necessary rigor. In the early days, the case was treated primarily as a missing persons case rather than a potential abduction, which some argue may have hampered the investigation.

The case took a significant turn in the summer of 2007 when the PJ declared Kate and Gerry McCann as "arguidos" (formal suspects). This development followed the discovery of what the police claimed was Madeleine's DNA in the trunk of a rental car the McCanns had hired 25 days after her disappearance. The McCanns vehemently denied any involvement, and the evidence was later discredited due to issues with contamination and the reliability of the forensic techniques used. In July 2008, the Portuguese attorney general archived the case, citing a lack of evidence to charge anyone, although it was stated that the case could be reopened if new evidence emerged.

The McCanns' response to their daughter's disappearance was marked by an unprecedented media campaign. They launched the "Find Madeleine" fund, which raised millions of pounds through public donations and various fundraising activities. This fund was used to finance their private investigations and maintain public awareness of the case. The McCanns also hired private investigators, who explored numerous leads and theories, including sightings of Madeleine across Europe and North Africa, potential trafficking, and abduction scenarios.

In 2011, the British Prime Minister, David Cameron, responding to a plea from the McCanns, instructed Scotland Yard to review the case. This led to the launch of Operation Grange, a multi-million-pound investigation aimed at examining the Portuguese case files, re-interviewing witnesses, and exploring new leads. Operation Grange initially worked under the hypothesis that Madeleine was abducted in a "criminal act by a stranger."

Over the years, Operation Grange has identified several persons of interest and lines of inquiry. One notable suspect was a German man named Christian Brückner, who was already imprisoned for unrelated crimes. In 2020, German prosecutors announced they had "concrete evidence" that Brückner was involved in Madeleine's disappearance, though they did not specify the nature of this evidence. Brückner had a history of sexual offenses against children and had lived in the Algarve region around the time Madeleine disappeared. Despite these assertions, no charges have been brought against him in relation to the case, and he has denied any involvement.

The disappearance of Madeleine McCann has generated a plethora of theories and speculation. Some believe she was abducted by a pedophile ring or human traffickers, while others think she might have been taken during a botched burglary. There are also those who believe Madeleine might still be alive, possibly living under a different identity. Numerous sightings and reported leads have emerged over the years, from Spain and Morocco to Australia and the United States, but none have led to Madeleine.

The impact of Madeleine's disappearance on her family has been profound and long-lasting. Kate and Gerry McCann have dedicated their lives to searching for their daughter, maintaining hope that she might still be found. They have faced intense scrutiny, with some critics accusing them of negligence for leaving their children alone that night. The McCanns have always defended their actions, insisting they were keeping a watchful eye and were only a short distance away. Their resilience and determination have been both admired and criticized, illustrating the complex emotional landscape surrounding the case.

The media coverage of Madeleine's disappearance has also been a topic of significant discussion. The case became a global news story, with extensive coverage in newspapers, television, and online platforms. This intense media focus brought widespread attention and support but also led to sensationalism and the spread of misinformation. The McCanns won libel cases against several British tabloids that had published false and defamatory stories about them, further highlighting the ethical challenges in reporting such sensitive cases.

In the broader context of missing persons cases, Madeleine's disappearance has had a notable impact on how such investigations are conducted. It highlighted the importance of international cooperation, the need for rapid and coordinated response protocols, and the critical role of media in both aiding and complicating investigations. The case has also spurred legislative and policy changes aimed at improving child protection and law enforcement practices.

Despite the passage of time, the search for Madeleine McCann continues. Advances in forensic science and technology offer hope that new evidence might one day emerge, providing answers to the questions that have haunted her family and the public for so long. The enduring mystery of what happened to Madeleine remains a poignant reminder of the pain and uncertainty faced by families of missing children and the unyielding human drive to seek truth and justice.

The disappearance of Madeleine McCann is a tragic story that combines elements of mystery, heartbreak, and the relentless pursuit of answers. It has captivated and confounded the world, becoming a symbol of both the fragility of life and the enduring strength of familial love and hope. As the investigation continues, the world watches, waiting for the day when the mystery may finally be resolved and Madeleine's story can be brought to a close.

Chapter 20: The Unsolved Murder of JonBenét Ramsey

The unsolved murder of JonBenét Ramsey remains one of the most perplexing and talked-about cases in American criminal history. JonBenét Patricia Ramsey was a six-year-old beauty queen who was found dead in her family's home in Boulder, Colorado, on December 26, 1996. The case has captivated public interest and sparked numerous theories, investigations, and debates over the decades. The circumstances surrounding her death, the handling of the investigation, and the myriads of suspects and theories contribute to its enduring mystery.

JonBenét was reported missing by her parents, Patsy and John Ramsey, in the early hours of December 26. Patsy discovered a ransom note demanding $118,000 for her daughter's return, a sum curiously close to John Ramsey's recent bonus. The note was written in a highly unusual style, with a mix of formal and informal language, leading to speculation about its authenticity. Despite the note's instructions, the police were called, and a search of the house was initiated. Eight hours later, John Ramsey discovered JonBenét's body in the basement. She had been garroted and suffered a severe blow to the head, with a nylon cord around her neck and wrists, and duct tape over her mouth.

The initial handling of the case by the Boulder Police Department was fraught with mistakes. The crime scene was not properly secured, and numerous people, including friends and family, were allowed to roam the house, potentially contaminating evidence. Critical errors included not immediately separating the parents for questioning and failing to conduct a thorough search of the house when they first arrived. These missteps significantly hampered the investigation and led to a cloud of suspicion over the family.

Early on, the Ramseys became the primary focus of the investigation. The unusual ransom note, the discovery of the body by John Ramsey, and Patsy's frantic 911 call raised suspicions. Some investigators believed the crime scene was staged to cover up an accidental death or a family member's involvement. However, the Ramseys maintained their innocence and pointed to an intruder theory, citing an unidentified boot print near JonBenét's body and an open window in the basement.

The media frenzy surrounding the case was unprecedented. The public was bombarded with speculation, leaked information, and sensational headlines. The Ramseys were scrutinized in the court of public opinion, with many believing their guilt based on circumstantial evidence and media portrayal. Tabloid newspapers and television shows capitalized on the public's morbid curiosity, often distorting facts and perpetuating rumors. The intense media coverage created a biased atmosphere that influenced public perception and possibly the investigation itself.

Numerous suspects and theories have emerged over the years. One theory involves a local man named Bill McReynolds, who played Santa Claus at a Christmas party held at the Ramseys' home just days before the murder. McReynolds had an unusual fascination with JonBenét, but he was ultimately cleared of any involvement. Another theory implicates a housekeeper, Linda Hoffmann-Pugh, who had financial troubles and allegedly asked the Ramseys for a loan shortly before the murder. However, she also was not charged due to lack of evidence.

In 2003, significant developments arose when forensic investigators discovered trace DNA on JonBenét's clothing that did not match any family members. This finding fueled the intruder theory, suggesting that an unknown male could have been responsible. Despite this, no match was found in the national DNA database, leaving the case unresolved.

In 2006, John Mark Karr, a former schoolteacher, falsely confessed to JonBenét's murder, providing explicit details about the crime. However, his confession was discredited when DNA evidence proved he was not the perpetrator. Karr's false confession further complicated the case, demonstrating how high-profile cases can attract individuals seeking attention or notoriety.

The grand jury convened in 1999 to review evidence in the case and voted to indict John and Patsy Ramsey on charges of child abuse resulting in death, but the district attorney declined to prosecute, citing insufficient evidence. This decision highlighted the ongoing conflict between law enforcement and prosecutorial authorities regarding the direction of the investigation.

In the years following the murder, John and Patsy Ramsey actively sought to clear their names, hiring private investigators and cooperating with media interviews. Patsy Ramsey passed away in 2006 from ovarian cancer, still under the cloud of suspicion. John Ramsey continued to advocate for further investigation into the case, emphasizing the intruder theory.

The JonBenét Ramsey case has also had a lasting impact on American culture and the field of criminal investigation. It exposed flaws in forensic and investigative procedures, influencing changes in how police handle crime scenes, manage media relations, and approach high-profile cases. The case also underscored the importance of preserving evidence, maintaining objectivity, and the potential pitfalls of public and media influence on criminal investigations.

Despite numerous documentaries, books, and articles examining the case, the murder of JonBenét Ramsey remains unsolved. Advances in forensic technology and investigative methods continue to offer hope that new evidence may one day emerge. The case serves as a reminder of the complexities and challenges inherent in solving crimes, particularly those shrouded in media sensationalism and public scrutiny. The search for JonBenét's killer persists, driven by a collective desire for justice and closure for a young life tragically cut short.

Chapter 21: The Axeman of New Orleans

The Axeman of New Orleans is a moniker attributed to an unidentified serial killer active in New Orleans, Louisiana, and surrounding communities, including Gretna, from May 1918 to October 1919. This notorious figure instilled widespread fear and hysteria through a series of brutal and seemingly random attacks, primarily targeting Italian-American grocers and their families. The nature of the crimes, the elusive identity of the killer, and the eerie circumstances surrounding the attacks have made the Axeman a legendary figure in the annals of American crime history.

The first recognized attack attributed to the Axeman occurred on May 23, 1918, when Joseph Maggio, an Italian grocer, and his wife, Catherine, were found brutally attacked in their apartment above their store. The perpetrator had broken into their home and attacked them with an axe, which belonged to the victims. Catherine's throat had been slit with a straight razor, and both she and her husband had suffered severe head injuries. Despite the grisly scene, the police found few clues to the killer's identity. A razor was found in the neighbor's yard, later traced to Andrew Maggio, Joseph's brother, who had a barbershop nearby. Although initially a suspect, Andrew was quickly cleared of involvement.

The murders continued in similar fashion over the following months. On June 28, 1918, Louis Besumer, another grocer, and his mistress, Harriet Lowe, were attacked in the early morning hours. Both victims survived but suffered serious injuries. Besumer was struck with an axe, and Lowe sustained a deep head wound. Lowe later accused Besumer of being a German spy, adding to the case's complexity. However, police dismissed her claims as unfounded.

The Axeman's reign of terror continued with the murder of Mrs. Mary Schneider on August 5, 1918, and the brutal attack on Pauline and Mary Bruno on August 10, 1918. The killer typically gained entry by chiseling out a panel on the back door and using the victims' own tools as weapons. This method of entry and the choice of weaponry were consistent across multiple crime scenes, pointing to the same perpetrator.

On March 10, 1919, the Axeman struck again, attacking the Cortimiglia family in Gretna. Charles Cortimiglia, his wife, Rosie, and their two-year-old daughter, Mary, were all assaulted with an axe. Tragically, young Mary did not survive. Rosie initially accused their neighbors, the Jordano family, of the crime, but her story was later discredited, and the charges were dropped. The attacks showed a pattern of targeting Italian immigrants, specifically grocers, which led to speculation that the crimes were racially motivated or linked to Mafia activity. However, these theories were never conclusively proven.

The most infamous aspect of the Axeman case was the letter purportedly sent by the killer to the New Orleans Times-Picayune on March 13, 1919. The letter, filled with bizarre and taunting language, claimed that the Axeman would spare any home where jazz music was being played at 12:15 a.m. on the night of March 19, 1919. This strange missive led to a citywide jazz playing frenzy, with dance halls, clubs, and private homes filled with music, as residents hoped to avoid the Axeman's wrath. The night passed without incident, further deepening the mystery and legend of the Axeman.

Despite extensive investigations, the Axeman was never caught. Various suspects were arrested and later released due to lack of evidence. Theories about the killer's identity ranged from a deranged local to an out-of-town criminal passing through New Orleans. The lack of concrete evidence, reliable witnesses, and consistent modus operandi left the police with little to go on.

One of the most peculiar aspects of the Axeman case is the blend of factual evidence and myth that surrounds it. The figure of the Axeman has become part of New Orleans' folklore, with many attributing supernatural or demonic qualities to the killer. This blending of myth and reality has only served to deepen the intrigue and fascination with the case.

Several factors contributed to the Axeman's success in evading capture. The early 20th century saw significant limitations in forensic science and investigative techniques. Fingerprinting was in its infancy, and DNA analysis was non-existent. Additionally, the Axeman's method of using the victims' own tools as weapons meant that no identifiable weapon was left at the crime scenes, complicating the search for tangible evidence.

The impact of the Axeman on New Orleans cannot be understated. The city was gripped by fear, and the Italian-American community, in particular, felt targeted and vulnerable. Newspapers sensationalized the murders, contributing to the panic and hysteria. The attacks also led to increased racial tension and suspicion within the community, as people sought to identify the mysterious killer in their midst.

The legacy of the Axeman lives on in popular culture. The story has been the subject of numerous books, articles, and documentaries, exploring the various aspects of the case and its enduring mystery. The Axeman has also been immortalized in music, most notably in the jazz song "The Mysterious Axman's Jazz (Don't Scare Me Papa)," which was inspired by the infamous letter to the Times-Picayune. The Axeman's tale was further popularized by its inclusion in the television series "American Horror Story: Coven," where the character was portrayed as a ghostly figure with a penchant for jazz music.

Despite the passage of time, the case of the Axeman of New Orleans remains one of the most chilling and enigmatic chapters in the history of American crime. The combination of brutal violence, eerie circumstances, and the killer's taunting letter to the press has ensured that the legend of the Axeman endures, continuing to capture the imagination of those fascinated by unsolved mysteries. The true identity of the Axeman remains unknown, a shadowy figure lurking in the annals of criminal history, leaving behind a legacy of fear and intrigue that endures to this day.

Chapter 22: The Disappearance of Flight MH370

The disappearance of Malaysia Airlines Flight MH370 is one of the most confounding and mysterious aviation incidents in history, sparking a plethora of theories, extensive search operations, and a multitude of unanswered questions. The Boeing 777-200ER, carrying 227 passengers and 12 crew members, vanished on March 8, 2014, while flying from Kuala Lumpur, Malaysia, to Beijing, China. Despite being one of the most technologically advanced aircraft of its time, MH370's disappearance has led to one of the most prolonged and expensive search efforts, yet the majority of the plane remains missing, leaving the fate of those aboard unknown.

MH370 took off from Kuala Lumpur International Airport at 12:41 a.m. local time and was scheduled to land in Beijing at 6:30 a.m. Initially, everything seemed routine. The plane reached its cruising altitude of 35,000 feet at 1:01 a.m. and communicated with air traffic control. However, at 1:19 a.m., the final voice communication from the cockpit, "Good night. Malaysian three-seven-zero," was heard. Shortly after this, at 1:21 a.m., the aircraft's transponder, which relays identifying information and altitude to radar, was switched off. Around the same time, MH370 deviated from its planned flight path, turning westward back over the Malay Peninsula.

Primary radar, used by military and some civilian installations, tracked the aircraft as it flew across the peninsula and turned southwest towards the Andaman Sea. At 2:22 a.m., the plane was last detected by Malaysian military radar over the Andaman Sea, northwest of Penang Island. After this point, MH370 disappeared from radar screens, entering an informational void that has led to intense speculation and investigation.

Initial searches focused on the South China Sea, based on the flight's last known position and intended path. However, with the revelation of the aircraft's deviation, search efforts shifted to the Andaman Sea and the Indian Ocean. The Australian Transport Safety Bureau (ATSB) led the search efforts in the southern Indian Ocean, focusing on an arc determined by satellite communications data, specifically Inmarsat's "handshake" pings. These pings indicated the aircraft's position along an arc at hourly intervals until 8:19 a.m., suggesting the plane had flown for approximately seven hours after losing contact with air traffic control.

The primary theory is that MH370 ended up in the southern Indian Ocean, far from any landmass. This conclusion was drawn from the analysis of satellite data, which indicated the aircraft's final position. However, pinpointing the exact crash site proved to be incredibly challenging due to the vast and remote nature of the search area, as well as the depth and terrain of the ocean floor. The initial search phase covered an area of around 120,000 square kilometers but yielded no significant results. The underwater search, using advanced technology like towed sonar and autonomous underwater vehicles, faced numerous difficulties, including adverse weather conditions and technical challenges.

On July 29, 2015, a significant breakthrough occurred when a piece of debris, later confirmed to be a flaperon from MH370, was found on the shores of Réunion Island in the Indian Ocean. This discovery provided the first tangible evidence that the aircraft had indeed crashed in the Indian Ocean. Subsequent debris, including parts of the wing and fuselage, was found on various western Indian Ocean islands and along the African coast. These findings, while crucial, were limited in number and did not offer enough information to reconstruct the flight's final moments comprehensively.

Multiple theories have been proposed regarding the disappearance of MH370, ranging from mechanical failure and pilot actions to hijacking and even more outlandish conspiracy theories. One leading theory suggests that a sudden catastrophic event, such as a fire or decompression, incapacitated the crew and passengers, leading to a "ghost flight" where the plane continued on autopilot until fuel exhaustion. Another theory posits that deliberate actions by the pilot or a hijacker led to the aircraft's diversion and eventual crash. Theories about mechanical failure consider the possibility of electrical or structural issues that may have rendered the crew incapable of managing the aircraft.

The pilot, Captain Zaharie Ahmad Shah, came under scrutiny due to his experience and knowledge. Some theorists suggest that he may have intentionally diverted the flight for reasons unknown, supported by evidence such as a simulated flight path on his home computer resembling the suspected route of MH370. However, no conclusive evidence has been found to confirm deliberate actions by Zaharie or any other crew member.

The disappearance of MH370 has also highlighted issues in international aviation safety and coordination. The lack of real-time aircraft tracking and the initial confusion and delay in the search efforts exposed significant gaps in the global air traffic control system. As a result, the International Civil Aviation Organization (ICAO) has since mandated the adoption of new standards for aircraft tracking, requiring planes to report their position every 15 minutes and every minute during distress.

The search for MH370 was officially suspended in January 2017 after nearly three years of extensive underwater search operations costing around $160 million, with no conclusive results. A private search effort funded by the company Ocean Infinity resumed in January 2018 but was also suspended after several months without success. Despite these setbacks, there remains a persistent call from families of the victims and aviation experts for continued search efforts, driven by the need for closure and understanding of what happened.

The disappearance of Malaysia Airlines Flight MH370 remains an enduring enigma in modern aviation history, symbolizing the limits of current technology and the vastness of our planet's unexplored regions. It stands as a somber reminder of the unknowns that still exist in an age where we often believe every corner of the globe is accessible and monitored. The mystery of MH370 has not only impacted the families of the passengers and crew but has also had a profound effect on aviation safety and search and rescue operations worldwide. The hope remains that one day, advancements in technology or new evidence will bring definitive answers to the fate of MH370, providing closure to one of the most perplexing aviation mysteries of all time.

Chapter 23: The Murder of Elizabeth Short

The murder of Elizabeth Short, widely known as the Black Dahlia, remains one of the most infamous unsolved cases in American criminal history. The case stands out not only because of the gruesome nature of the crime but also due to the intense media frenzy it generated, the myriads of theories and suspects it produced, and its lasting impact on popular culture.

Elizabeth Short was born on July 29, 1924, in Hyde Park, Massachusetts. She moved to California in the mid-1940s, seeking fame and a career in Hollywood, like many young women of her era. Short lived a transient lifestyle, moving frequently and working various odd jobs. She was described as an attractive woman with striking dark hair, often dressed in black, which later contributed to her posthumous nickname, the Black Dahlia.

On January 15, 1947, Short's mutilated body was discovered in a vacant lot in the Leimert Park neighborhood of Los Angeles. The horrific state of her remains shocked even seasoned investigators. Short had been bisected at the waist, with both halves of her body posed in a spread-eagle fashion. Her face had been severely mutilated, with cuts extending from the corners of her mouth to her ears, creating a macabre "Glasgow smile." There were numerous cuts and abrasions on her breasts and thighs, and her body had been drained of blood, leaving the skin pale and waxy. Despite the brutality of the crime, no blood was found at the scene, suggesting that she had been killed elsewhere and her body meticulously cleaned before being dumped.

The investigation into Elizabeth Short's murder was immediately hampered by the sheer volume of media coverage. Newspapers sensationalized the case, dubbing Short the "Black Dahlia" and publishing lurid details about her life and death. The Los Angeles

Police Department (LAPD) was inundated with tips and confessions, many of which proved to be false leads. Over the years, more than 500 people have confessed to the murder, including several women, but none of these confessions have been substantiated.

The LAPD's investigation initially focused on Short's personal life, interviewing friends, acquaintances, and anyone who had contact with her in the weeks leading up to her death. They uncovered a picture of a young woman who was both charming and enigmatic, often struggling financially and relying on the generosity of friends and acquaintances for support. Short was known to frequent nightclubs and bars, and she had a reputation for being friendly but also reserved about her personal life.

One of the early suspects in the case was Robert "Red" Manley, a salesman who had been one of the last people to see Short alive. Manley had given Short a ride from San Diego to Los Angeles and checked her into the Biltmore Hotel on January 9, 1947. He was initially cooperative with the police, providing details of their time together and submitting to a polygraph test, which he passed. Despite extensive questioning, Manley was eventually cleared of any involvement in the murder.

As the investigation progressed, several theories emerged about who might have been responsible for the brutal killing. Some investigators believed the murder had been the work of a deranged individual with medical knowledge, given the precise nature of the bisection and the surgical techniques used. This theory led to scrutiny of several medical professionals in the area, but no solid evidence was found to implicate any of them.

Another theory suggested that Short's murder was linked to the criminal underworld of Los Angeles. The 1940s saw significant organized crime activity in the city, and it was speculated that Short may have crossed paths with someone involved in these circles.

However, no concrete connections to organized crime were ever established.

One of the most compelling suspects to emerge in later years was George Hodel, a wealthy and prominent Los Angeles physician. Hodel's own son, Steve Hodel, a retired LAPD homicide detective, has extensively investigated his father's possible involvement in the Black Dahlia murder. Steve Hodel's book, "Black Dahlia Avenger," presents evidence that his father had both the medical expertise and the psychological profile to commit the crime. George Hodel was known for his unconventional lifestyle and connections to the artistic and intellectual elite of Los Angeles. He had been investigated for other crimes, including the sexual assault of his own daughter, but was never charged with Short's murder. The Hodel residence, known as the Sowden House, was a place of interest in the investigation, with some suggesting it could have been the site of Short's murder.

Despite the compelling nature of the evidence against George Hodel, including photographs and entries in his journal that seem to suggest knowledge of the crime, there remains no definitive proof linking him to the murder. The LAPD has neither confirmed nor denied Hodel's involvement, leaving his alleged connection to the case open to speculation.

The murder of Elizabeth Short has continued to fascinate and horrify the public for decades. Numerous books, films, and television shows have been inspired by the case, each offering different interpretations and theories. James Ellroy's novel "The Black Dahlia," later adapted into a film by Brian De Palma, is a fictionalized account of the case that captures the dark allure and mystery surrounding Short's life and death.

The case also had a significant impact on the investigation and prosecution of homicides in Los Angeles. The intense media scrutiny and public pressure forced the LAPD to adopt more sophisticated forensic techniques and investigative methods. The Black Dahlia case is often cited as a catalyst for improvements in how high-profile cases are handled, including better management of crime scenes and more strategic communication with the media.

Despite the passage of time, the case remains open, with the LAPD periodically reviewing new evidence and leads. The advent of new forensic technologies, such as DNA analysis, offers a glimmer of hope that the mystery might one day be solved. However, the lack of preserved evidence from the original investigation poses a significant challenge to any modern efforts to conclusively identify Short's killer.

Elizabeth Short's legacy is a complex blend of victimhood and myth. She has become an icon of Hollywood's dark underbelly, a symbol of the era's dreams and dangers. Her murder serves as a grim reminder of the vulnerabilities faced by young women pursuing fame and fortune in a city that can be both glamorous and unforgiving. The enduring fascination with her case reflects broader societal obsessions with beauty, crime, and the macabre, ensuring that the mystery of the Black Dahlia will continue to captivate the public imagination for years to come.

Chapter 24: The Overtoun Bridge Dog Deaths

The Overtoun Bridge dog deaths constitute one of the most bizarre and mysterious phenomena in Scotland's history, intriguing locals, visitors, and paranormal enthusiasts alike. Located near Dumbarton, the Overtoun Bridge has been the site of unexplained incidents where numerous dogs have seemingly committed suicide by leaping off the bridge, plunging 50 feet to their deaths in the ravine below. This strange occurrence, which has been reported since the 1950s, has led to various theories ranging from natural explanations to supernatural forces.

The Overtoun Bridge, constructed in 1895, is a beautiful stone structure that forms part of the Overtoun Estate, an area rich in history and scenic beauty. The bridge spans a deep ravine with a stream known as the Overtoun Burn flowing beneath it. The estate includes the Overtoun House, a Victorian mansion built in 1862 by industrialist James White. The area is imbued with a sense of mystery and legend, contributing to the eerie aura surrounding the bridge.

Reports of dogs leaping from the bridge began in the mid-20th century and have continued sporadically since then. Estimates suggest that between 50 and 600 dogs have leapt from the bridge, with many dying from the fall and others sustaining severe injuries. The incidents predominantly involve long-nosed breeds such as collies, retrievers, and Labradors, which has added another layer of curiosity to the mystery. The jumps almost exclusively occur from one specific side of the bridge, usually during clear, dry weather, and always at a particular spot between the last two parapets.

Several theories have been proposed to explain these perplexing events. One of the leading natural explanations involves the presence of strong scents emitted by animals in the ravine below. Dr. David Sands, an animal behaviorist, conducted an investigation and found that the area beneath the bridge is home to numerous small mammals, such as mink, squirrels, and mice. These animals produce potent odors that could potentially attract dogs, especially breeds with a strong sense of smell. Sands posited that the dogs, captivated by the scents, might leap over the parapet without realizing the height of the drop on the other side.

Another theory suggests that the unique design of the bridge itself could be a contributing factor. The structure features tall granite walls that prevent dogs from seeing the drop until it is too late. Coupled with the fact that dogs have a different visual perspective compared to humans, it is plausible that they might misjudge the height and jump, expecting to land on solid ground.

Some locals and paranormal enthusiasts believe that the bridge is haunted or influenced by supernatural forces. The Overtoun Estate has long been associated with folklore and legends. One popular legend is that of the "Thin Place," a Celtic belief in a location where the barrier between the physical world and the spiritual realm is thin. According to this legend, Overtoun Bridge is one such thin place, where dogs might be more susceptible to sensing or reacting to otherworldly presences.

Adding to the supernatural theories is the story of a tragic event in the 1990s. In 1994, a local man named Kevin Moy threw his infant son from the bridge, claiming that his child was the incarnation of the Devil. Moy then attempted to take his own life by jumping off the bridge but survived. This horrific incident has fueled beliefs that the bridge is cursed or possesses a malevolent force that drives beings to commit suicide.

Despite these theories, no definitive explanation has been universally accepted. The phenomena have drawn the attention of various researchers, animal psychologists, and paranormal investigators, each providing different perspectives but no concrete answers. The mystery remains unsolved, leaving room for continued speculation and investigation.

The Overtoun Bridge dog deaths have also had a significant impact on the local community. Signs have been erected near the bridge, warning dog owners to keep their pets on a leash while crossing. Local authorities and animal welfare organizations have been involved in raising awareness about the potential dangers associated with the bridge. The incidents have also influenced the perception of the Overtoun Estate, with many visitors now viewing it as a place of eerie fascination rather than just historical interest.

The case of the Overtoun Bridge dog deaths has permeated popular culture, inspiring articles, documentaries, and even episodes of television shows exploring the paranormal. The bridge's grim reputation as a "dog suicide bridge" has attracted tourists and curiosity-seekers, further embedding it into the folklore of the region.

Chapter 25: The Mystery of the Lead Masks Case

The mystery of the Lead Masks Case is one of the most perplexing and bizarre unsolved cases in Brazilian history, involving the deaths of two electronic technicians, Manoel Pereira da Cruz and Miguel José Viana, under mysterious circumstances. The case, which occurred in 1966, has intrigued and baffled investigators, journalists, and paranormal enthusiasts alike due to its strange details and lack of clear answers.

On August 20, 1966, the bodies of Cruz and Viana were discovered on the Morro do Vintém hill in Niterói, Rio de Janeiro. A local teenager named Jorge da Costa Alves, who was flying a kite, stumbled upon the corpses and alerted the authorities. When the police arrived, they found the bodies lying next to each other, partially covered by grass. Both men were dressed in formal suits, wore lead eye masks, and had waterproof coats. Next to the bodies, police found an empty water bottle and a notebook containing cryptic instructions, including phrases like "16:30 be at the specified location," "18:30 ingest capsules, after effect protect metals wait for mask signal."

The discovery of the lead masks immediately captured public and media attention due to their unusual nature. These masks were simple, crudely cut pieces of lead, which appeared to be intended to protect the wearers' eyes from something. The inclusion of the masks led to various speculations, including theories involving extraterrestrial encounters, secret scientific experiments, and religious rituals. The mysterious instructions in the notebook further deepened the intrigue, suggesting that the men were following a precise plan that involved taking capsules at a specific time.

Cruz and Viana were both known to be interested in electronics and had reportedly been working on building a device to communicate with extraterrestrial beings. Some friends and relatives mentioned that the men were part of a group interested in spiritualism and believed in contacting beings from other planets. This background information fueled the theory that the deaths were related to an attempt to make such contact, possibly involving hallucinogenic drugs to enhance their experience.

Autopsies on the bodies were inconclusive due to the advanced state of decomposition, as several days had passed since their deaths. Toxicological analyses could not be performed, as the internal organs were too decomposed to provide useful samples. This inability to determine the presence of any drugs or toxins in their system left a significant gap in understanding what might have caused their deaths. There were no obvious signs of violence or struggle, and the cause of death remained undetermined, leading to rampant speculation.

One theory posits that Cruz and Viana died from poisoning or overdose after ingesting the capsules mentioned in the notebook. The precise nature of these capsules is unknown, but they could have been some form of psychoactive substance or poison. Given their interest in spiritualism and extraterrestrial contact, it is possible that they consumed these capsules as part of a ritual or experiment. However, without toxicological evidence, this remains speculative.

Another theory involves the lead masks themselves. Some have suggested that the masks were intended to protect the men from radiation or some other harmful effect during their experiment. However, there is no concrete evidence that they were exposed to any dangerous substances, and the purpose of the masks remains a mystery. The inclusion of lead masks in this scenario is unusual and does not align with any known practices or technologies.

The involvement of a third party has also been considered. Some investigators theorized that the men were led to the hill and poisoned by someone else, possibly as part of a scam or due to a disagreement within their group. This theory is supported by the fact that no other similar incidents were reported, suggesting that their deaths were not a result of widespread practice or phenomenon. However, there were no signs of a struggle or forced ingestion, making it difficult to support this hypothesis definitively.

The lack of clear evidence and the unusual circumstances surrounding the deaths have led to numerous speculative and fantastical theories. Some suggest that Cruz and Viana were involved in a government or military experiment gone wrong, possibly related to mind control or other covert operations. Others believe that they were the victims of a cult or secret society, conducting rituals that required their deaths. These theories, while intriguing, lack substantive evidence and are often dismissed as sensationalism.

The media coverage of the Lead Masks Case played a significant role in shaping public perception and fueling speculation. Newspapers and television programs at the time were quick to highlight the most bizarre and sensational aspects of the case, often without thorough investigation. This led to a proliferation of myths and rumors, which have persisted over the decades. The case has been featured in numerous books, documentaries, and articles, each offering different interpretations and adding to the overall mystery.

Despite extensive investigation by the local police and attention from various researchers, the Lead Masks Case remains unsolved. The lack of concrete evidence, the ambiguous nature of the clues, and the passage of time have made it increasingly difficult to uncover the truth. The case is now considered a classic unsolved mystery, often cited in discussions of unexplained phenomena and bizarre deaths.

In the years following the discovery of the bodies, several similar incidents were reported, although none were as well-documented or as mysterious as the Lead Masks Case. These subsequent cases involved individuals found dead in unusual circumstances, often with cryptic notes or items suggesting involvement in secretive or experimental activities. While these cases are often compared to the Lead Masks Case, they have not provided any additional insights or breakthroughs.

The mystery of the Lead Masks Case continues to captivate those interested in the unexplained. It serves as a reminder of the limitations of investigative techniques, especially when dealing with unusual and ambiguous evidence. The case also highlights the human fascination with the unknown and the lengths to which people will go to seek answers, even when faced with seemingly insurmountable challenges. As long as the case remains unsolved, it will continue to be a source of speculation, curiosity, and intrigue, embodying the enduring allure of the mysterious and the unknown.

Chapter 26: The Isdal Woman Enigma

The Isdal Woman enigma is one of Norway's most haunting and perplexing unsolved mysteries. It involves the discovery of a woman's burned body in the remote Isdalen Valley near Bergen on November 29, 1970. The case has baffled investigators for decades, spawning numerous theories and speculations about the identity of the woman, the circumstances of her death, and the possible reasons behind the numerous strange elements surrounding the case.

The story begins when a professor and his two daughters, hiking in the Isdalen Valley, stumbled upon the charred remains of a woman hidden among the rocks. The police were called, and a detailed examination of the scene revealed several puzzling details. The woman had suffered extensive burns, and her body was found in a supine position, with her head pointing towards a cliff. Scattered around the site were various personal items, including an empty bottle of St. Hallvard liqueur, two plastic water bottles, a partially burned passport, a broken umbrella, a fur hat, and some pieces of jewelry, all of which had their identifying marks removed. This meticulous effort to erase the woman's identity was one of the first indications that the case was not a simple accident or random crime.

Initial forensic analysis indicated that the woman had died from a combination of burns and carbon monoxide poisoning, suggesting that she was alive when she was set on fire. Further examination revealed a significant amount of phenobarbital, a strong sedative, in her system. Additionally, investigators found traces of petrol on her body and belongings, reinforcing the theory that she had been deliberately burned.

The lack of identification documents and the removal of labels from her clothing presented a major challenge for the police. They issued an Interpol alert and conducted extensive checks across Europe, but no matches were found for missing persons. The only clues to her identity were several suitcases discovered in a storage facility at the Bergen railway station, which were linked to the woman through fingerprints. These suitcases contained clothing, cosmetics, wigs, and a notepad with numeric codes, later determined to be dates and places. Among the contents was also a prescription for a lotion, but the doctor's name and the patient's details had been removed.

Investigators soon discovered that the Isdal Woman had used at least eight different aliases during her travels across Europe, including names like Claudia Tielt and Vera Jarle. She had stayed in several hotels in Norway, always registering under different names and claiming to be Belgian or from South America. Witnesses described her as a well-dressed, elegant woman, fluent in several languages, including French, German, and broken English. Her behavior was noted to be secretive and unusual, often changing rooms after checking in and requesting specific views.

The coded notepad found in her luggage revealed a pattern of travel that suggested she had been on some sort of mission or assignment. The codes, once deciphered, corresponded to dates and locations of her stays in various European cities, primarily in Norway. This, coupled with her use of multiple identities, led to widespread speculation that she might have been involved in espionage. The Cold War context of the time further fueled these suspicions, as Norway, with its strategic location and NATO membership, was a hotspot for intelligence activities.

Despite exhaustive efforts, the true identity of the Isdal Woman and the purpose of her travels remained elusive. Inquiries with embassies, airlines, and shipping companies yielded no conclusive leads. The possibility of her being a spy was considered plausible, given her secretive behavior, multiple identities, and the presence of sophisticated disguises. Some speculated that she could have been involved in industrial or political espionage, possibly working for either the Eastern or Western blocs. However, there was no concrete evidence to support these theories.

Another line of inquiry explored the possibility of the Isdal Woman being involved in illegal activities such as drug trafficking or organized crime. The phenobarbital in her system suggested she might have been a habitual user of sedatives, potentially pointing to a connection with the criminal underworld. Yet, no direct links to known criminal organizations were found, and her refined appearance and behavior seemed inconsistent with typical drug mules or low-level operatives.

The case took another twist with the discovery of two Belgian men who had been seen with the Isdal Woman in Bergen shortly before her death. They were interviewed by the police but denied any knowledge of her identity or circumstances. Their connection to her, if any, remained unclear, adding another layer of mystery to the case.

In recent years, advances in forensic technology have reignited interest in the Isdal Woman case. In 2016, Norwegian police reopened the investigation, employing modern techniques such as isotope analysis to determine her geographical origins. The results indicated that she likely spent her early years in central or eastern Europe, possibly in a German-speaking region. This finding, while intriguing, did not significantly narrow down the search for her identity.

The enigmatic nature of the Isdal Woman case has inspired numerous books, documentaries, and podcasts, each exploring different theories and angles. Some suggest that she might have been a defector or an informant whose cover was blown, leading to her murder. Others propose that she was the victim of a personal vendetta or a crime of passion, killed by someone who knew her true identity. Yet, there are those who believe that her death was a result of a botched intelligence operation, with her handlers eliminating her to prevent exposure.

The Isdal Woman's story continues to captivate the public imagination, symbolizing the unresolved mysteries of the Cold War era. Her death, shrouded in secrecy and marked by a deliberate effort to erase her identity, raises profound questions about the nature of her life and the forces that led to her untimely demise. The case remains a poignant reminder of the human cost of clandestine activities and the enduring allure of unsolved mysteries.

Chapter 27: The Chicago Tylenol Murders

The Chicago Tylenol Murders represent one of the most chilling and impactful cases of product tampering in American history, fundamentally changing how over-the-counter medications are packaged and marketed. The case began in late September 1982, when seven people in the Chicago metropolitan area died after ingesting Tylenol capsules that had been laced with potassium cyanide. The deaths led to widespread panic, a massive recall of Tylenol products, and an intensive investigation that ultimately failed to identify the perpetrator.

The first victim, Mary Kellerman, a 12-year-old girl from Elk Grove Village, Illinois, fell ill on the morning of September 29, 1982, after taking Extra-Strength Tylenol to alleviate a sore throat and runny nose. She was rushed to the hospital but was pronounced dead shortly after arrival. That same day, Adam Janus, a 27-year-old postal worker from Arlington Heights, collapsed and died after taking Tylenol for chest pain. In a tragic twist, Adam's brother Stanley and his wife Theresa, grieving his sudden death, also took Tylenol from the same bottle and died.

As more deaths were reported, it became clear that these incidents were not isolated. Within days, investigators identified the common link between the victims: they had all consumed Tylenol capsules. The other victims included Mary Reiner, a 27-year-old who had just given birth; Paula Prince, a 35-year-old flight attendant; Mary McFarland, a 31-year-old from Elmhurst; and Mary Weiner, a 25-year-old from Winfield. The sudden and seemingly random nature of the deaths created a wave of fear and confusion throughout the Chicago area and beyond.

The discovery that the Tylenol capsules had been tampered with led to an immediate and widespread recall of the product by its manufacturer, Johnson & Johnson. The company, in a move that would later be lauded for its transparency and consumer-first approach, issued warnings through the media, urging the public to avoid using Tylenol products. They also set up hotlines and offered refunds to customers who had purchased the product. Johnson & Johnson's swift response was crucial in mitigating further harm and restoring public trust in the brand.

The recall involved approximately 31 million bottles of Tylenol, valued at over $100 million. Johnson & Johnson faced significant financial losses and a potential irreparable damage to its reputation. However, the company's decisive actions, including a complete recall and cooperation with law enforcement, were instrumental in managing the crisis. They later introduced tamper-evident packaging, which became a standard across the pharmaceutical industry, including foil seals and child-proof caps, to prevent similar incidents in the future.

The investigation into the Tylenol murders was massive, involving local, state, and federal agencies, including the FBI and the Food and Drug Administration (FDA). Investigators examined every aspect of the victims' lives to find a connection that could lead them to the perpetrator. They also scrutinized the supply chain of Tylenol, from the manufacturing plants to the retail outlets, to determine how the capsules had been contaminated.

Early theories suggested that the cyanide might have been introduced at the production level, but this was quickly ruled out as the contaminated bottles were found to come from different production lots. This led investigators to conclude that the tampering had occurred at the retail level, after the bottles had left the factory. The tamperer had apparently purchased bottles of Tylenol, laced the capsules with cyanide, and then returned the poisoned bottles to store shelves.

One of the most significant leads in the case came from a letter sent to Johnson & Johnson, demanding $1 million to stop the cyanide attacks. The letter was traced to James William Lewis, a man with a history of criminal activity, including fraud and extortion. Lewis was arrested and charged with extortion, but he denied any involvement in the actual poisonings. Despite extensive interrogation and investigation, there was insufficient evidence to link him directly to the murders, and he was never charged with the killings. Lewis served time for the extortion attempt but maintained his innocence regarding the murders.

The lack of concrete evidence and the inability to identify a clear suspect left the case unsolved. Despite the exhaustive efforts of law enforcement, the identity and motive of the Tylenol killer remain unknown. The FBI continued to investigate leads for years, re-examining the case periodically and utilizing new forensic techniques as they became available, but no definitive breakthroughs were achieved.

The impact of the Tylenol murders extended far beyond the immediate tragedy. The incident led to a complete overhaul of packaging practices for over-the-counter medications and many other consumer products. The introduction of tamper-evident packaging became a critical measure to ensure consumer safety and restore public confidence in the safety of everyday products. This change had a lasting effect on the industry, setting new standards for packaging and leading to the widespread adoption of safety seals and packaging innovations designed to prevent tampering.

Johnson & Johnson's handling of the crisis is often cited as a model for effective corporate crisis management. The company's transparency, prompt action, and focus on consumer safety helped it recover from a potentially devastating blow. Within a year, Tylenol had regained much of its market share, and Johnson & Johnson's reputation as a trusted brand was largely restored.

The Tylenol murders also had a significant cultural impact, highlighting the vulnerability of consumers and the potential for malicious tampering of everyday products. The case raised public awareness about product safety and led to stricter regulations and oversight by government agencies such as the FDA. It also prompted other industries to reevaluate their packaging and security measures to prevent similar incidents.

In the years following the Tylenol murders, there were several copycat incidents, where individuals attempted to tamper with consumer products in a similar manner. These incidents, although fewer in number and less deadly, reinforced the need for vigilance and stringent safety protocols. The legacy of the Tylenol murders continues to influence public health policies and practices, serving as a stark reminder of the potential for deliberate harm in the consumer marketplace.

Despite the passage of time, the case remains an open investigation. Advances in forensic science, such as DNA analysis and other modern techniques, hold the potential for new breakthroughs, but so far, they have not provided conclusive evidence to solve the case. The unsolved nature of the Tylenol murders continues to captivate the public and law enforcement, leaving many questions unanswered and serving as an enduring mystery in American criminal history.

Chapter 28: The Phantom Barber of Pascagoula

The Phantom Barber of Pascagoula is a notorious figure from the early 1940s, whose mysterious and unsettling activities have captivated and perplexed the residents of Pascagoula, Mississippi, and beyond. The series of bizarre break-ins, which involved an unidentified intruder cutting the hair of sleeping victims, remain one of the most peculiar and chilling unsolved mysteries in American criminal history. The Phantom Barber's reign of terror began in June 1942, during the height of World War II, and lasted for several months, leaving the community gripped with fear and speculation.

Pascagoula, a small and relatively quiet town, was suddenly thrust into a state of unease when reports emerged of an unknown assailant sneaking into homes and cutting the hair of unsuspecting residents. The first known incident occurred on the night of June 5, 1942, when two young girls, Mary Evelyn Briggs and Edna Marie Hydel, were targeted while they slept in their bedroom. Their mother discovered the strange occurrence the next morning: both girls had had significant portions of their hair cut off during the night, yet they were otherwise unharmed and had no recollection of the intrusion. This strange and seemingly harmless act was just the beginning of a series of similar incidents that would soon escalate.

As the summer progressed, more reports surfaced of the Phantom Barber's nocturnal activities. Victims ranged in age and gender, although young girls seemed to be the primary targets. Each time, the assailant would enter through a window, using stealth and precision to avoid waking the occupants. In one case, a young woman named Carol Petterson awoke to find her hair being cut and saw a shadowy figure fleeing the scene. Despite the clear invasion of privacy and the unsettling nature of these attacks, the Phantom Barber initially appeared to be more of a nuisance than a serious threat, as no one was physically harmed.

The community's anxiety grew as the bizarre intrusions continued, with the Phantom Barber seemingly able to strike at will, evading capture despite increased vigilance and police patrols. The local authorities were baffled by the intruder's ability to enter homes undetected and carry out the strange acts of hair-cutting. The town implemented various security measures, with residents securing their homes more rigorously and staying on high alert, but the Phantom Barber remained elusive.

The mystery deepened when the Phantom Barber's activities escalated from mere hair-cutting to more aggressive behavior. One notable incident involved a man named Terrell Cochran, who was attacked in his home. Cochran awoke to find a shadowy figure standing over his bed, and in the ensuing struggle, he sustained a blow to the head. Though Cochran survived the attack, the escalation in violence marked a significant shift in the Phantom Barber's modus operandi, raising concerns that the intruder might become even more dangerous.

The most severe incident attributed to the Phantom Barber occurred in August 1942, involving the Tonn family. Mr. and Mrs. Tonn were attacked in their home, with Mrs. Tonn suffering a severe head injury from a blunt instrument. This violent episode caused widespread panic, leading many to believe that the Phantom Barber had evolved from a peculiar prankster into a serious threat. The increased severity of the attacks prompted the police to intensify their efforts to apprehend the perpetrator, conducting extensive investigations and questioning numerous suspects, but the Phantom Barber's identity remained a mystery.

Several theories emerged regarding the Phantom Barber's motives and identity. Some speculated that the intrusions were the work of a mentally disturbed individual with a hair fetish, while others believed that the acts were part of a more sinister plot, possibly involving espionage or sabotage given the wartime context. Pascagoula was home to several wartime industries, including shipyards and manufacturing plants, leading some to suspect that the Phantom Barber might be a foreign agent or saboteur seeking to destabilize the community.

One suspect who garnered significant attention was a German chemist named William Dolan. Dolan had previously been involved in a legal dispute with a local family and was considered eccentric by many in the community. He was arrested in August 1942 after police found a hair sample in his possession that allegedly matched hair from one of the victims. Dolan was charged with attempted murder in connection with the attack on the Tonn family and was convicted based on circumstantial evidence. However, doubts about his guilt persisted, and many believed that Dolan was a convenient scapegoat rather than the true Phantom Barber. His conviction did little to alleviate the fear and uncertainty that had gripped Pascagoula.

Despite Dolan's arrest, the strange intrusions ceased, leading some to believe that the true Phantom Barber might have fled or ceased activities for fear of being caught. Others speculated that the perpetrator might have been someone with close ties to the community, who had successfully hidden in plain sight. The lack of concrete evidence and the unresolved nature of the case ensured that the mystery endured, becoming a subject of local folklore and intrigue.

The case of the Phantom Barber has since been studied by criminologists, historians, and paranormal enthusiasts, each offering various interpretations and theories. Some suggest that the Phantom Barber's activities were an early example of a serial offender who gained satisfaction from the act of intrusion and control over his victims, while others view the case through the lens of wartime paranoia and the social anxieties of the period.

In recent years, advances in forensic science and criminal profiling have led to renewed interest in the case, although no definitive answers have been uncovered. The Phantom Barber's identity and motives remain shrouded in mystery, and the case continues to be a topic of speculation and debate among those fascinated by unsolved crimes.

The legacy of the Phantom Barber of Pascagoula is one of eerie fascination and lingering fear. The case stands as a stark reminder of how even seemingly minor and inexplicable acts of intrusion can disrupt a community's sense of security and well-being. The Phantom Barber's ability to evade capture and the enduring mystery of his identity serve as a testament to the complexities and challenges of criminal investigation, particularly in an era before modern forensic techniques.

Chapter 29: The Death Valley Germans

The Death Valley Germans case is a chilling and tragic tale that involves the mysterious disappearance and eventual discovery of a German family in one of the most inhospitable environments in the United States: Death Valley. In the summer of 1996, a German family consisting of Egbert Rimkus, his girlfriend Cornelia "Conny" Meyer, and Egbert's son Georg Weber, along with Conny's son Max Meyer, embarked on a road trip across the American Southwest. This journey, intended to be a holiday adventure, ended in a tragedy that would perplex and haunt investigators and enthusiasts for years.

The family arrived in the United States with a well-thought-out itinerary, planning to visit various national parks and attractions. They rented a green Plymouth Voyager minivan in Los Angeles and set off on their journey, visiting Las Vegas and various sites around Southern California. However, things took a fateful turn when they entered the vast and unforgiving expanse of Death Valley. The region, known for its extreme temperatures and rugged terrain, is not to be taken lightly, especially during the height of summer when temperatures can soar well above 100 degrees Fahrenheit.

On July 22, 1996, the last known sighting of the family occurred at a gas station in Independence, California. They purchased fuel and were seen purchasing two gallons of water, a seemingly trivial but crucial detail given the environment they were about to enter. Shortly afterward, they ventured into Death Valley, a decision that proved disastrous. Despite the inhospitable nature of the desert, the family seemed ill-prepared for such an environment. They lacked sufficient supplies, particularly water, and there is no indication that they had a detailed understanding of the risks associated with traversing such a harsh landscape.

The family's journey into the desert became even more perplexing when it was discovered that they had deviated from known paths and trails. They entered the region via a remote and unpaved road called Anvil Spring Canyon Road, a route not commonly used by tourists. This route took them deep into the desert, far from any sources of help or support. The reasoning behind their choice to venture into such a remote area remains unclear. It is speculated that they may have been seeking a shortcut or a more adventurous path, but without any prior experience or adequate preparation, their decision was perilous.

As days passed without any contact from the family, concerns grew among friends and relatives back in Germany. On October 21, 1996, the rented minivan was discovered abandoned in a remote part of Death Valley, specifically near the edge of Anvil Spring Canyon. The vehicle was stuck in a rut, suggesting that the family had encountered difficulties with the terrain. Inside the van, investigators found an empty water bottle, a sleeping bag, and personal belongings, but no trace of the family themselves. The lack of footprints or other signs around the vehicle further deepened the mystery.

The discovery of the van initiated a massive search operation, involving both local authorities and volunteers. Despite extensive efforts, no signs of the family were found at the time. The harsh and expansive nature of Death Valley made the search challenging, with vast areas of treacherous terrain, dangerous heat, and limited water sources. The case eventually went cold, with many speculating that the family had succumbed to the elements and their bodies lost in the vastness of the desert.

It wasn't until years later that the case saw a significant breakthrough. In November 2009, Tom Mahood and Les Walker, amateur sleuths intrigued by the case, undertook an expedition into the Death Valley wilderness. Their interest was piqued by the lack of closure and the mystery surrounding the case. In a remote area, they discovered skeletal remains along with personal items that were later identified as belonging to the missing family. The remains were scattered, indicating that the family members had died at different times and possibly under different circumstances. The items found included identification documents and other personal effects, which provided a heartbreaking confirmation of the family's fate.

The discovery of the remains shed some light on the tragic end of the Death Valley Germans, but many questions remained unanswered. Why did they venture so far off the beaten path? Were they aware of the dangers they faced? The absence of clear information about their intentions and decisions continues to fuel speculation. Some theories suggest that they may have been misled by maps or misunderstood the terrain, while others propose that they may have been searching for a specific site or experience. The extreme conditions of the desert, combined with their apparent lack of preparation, undoubtedly played a critical role in their demise.

The Death Valley Germans case serves as a poignant reminder of the dangers of underestimating nature's power and the importance of preparation when venturing into unfamiliar and hostile environments. It also highlights the tragic consequences that can arise from a simple misjudgment or lack of information. While the case is largely considered solved with the identification of the remains, it remains a haunting example of how a seemingly ordinary vacation can turn into a fatal journey. The story of the Death Valley Germans continues to be a subject of fascination and sorrow, illustrating the profound and sometimes perilous allure of the American wilderness.

Chapter 30: The Unresolved Death of Edgar Allan Poe

The unresolved death of Edgar Allan Poe, one of America's most celebrated literary figures, is a topic that has captivated scholars, historians, and fans for over a century and a half. Poe, best known for his macabre and Gothic tales like "The Tell-Tale Heart," "The Fall of the House of Usher," and the poem "The Raven," was a pioneering figure in American literature, credited with inventing the detective fiction genre and contributing significantly to science fiction and horror. Despite his literary achievements, his life was fraught with hardship, poverty, and personal turmoil, culminating in his mysterious and untimely death at the age of 40.

On October 3, 1849, Poe was found in a state of delirium on the streets of Baltimore, Maryland. He was discovered outside Ryan's Tavern (sometimes referred to as Gunner's Hall), a polling place on Election Day. Joseph W. Walker, a compositor for the Baltimore Sun, was the one who found Poe and described him as being "in great distress, and... in need of immediate assistance." Poe was taken to the Washington College Hospital, where he remained in a state of semi-consciousness for four days before dying on October 7, 1849. The circumstances of his discovery, combined with his erratic behavior and the cryptic nature of his final days, have led to numerous theories and speculations regarding the cause of his death.

One of the earliest and most enduring theories is that Poe was a victim of "cooping," a form of electoral fraud practiced in the 19th century. In cooping, gangs would kidnap individuals, force them to vote multiple times for a particular candidate, often disguising them in different clothes and sometimes administering drugs or alcohol to ensure compliance. Poe was found on Election Day, wearing clothes that were not his own, which some have taken as evidence supporting the cooping theory. Additionally, his state of delirium and the lack of any coherent account of his activities in the days leading up to his discovery fit the pattern of a cooping victim.

Another prominent theory is that Poe succumbed to alcoholism. Poe had a well-documented history of alcohol abuse, exacerbated by his difficult life circumstances, including the early deaths of his mother, foster mother, and wife, Virginia Clemm. Accounts from those who knew Poe suggest that he had a low tolerance for alcohol and would become heavily intoxicated with even small amounts. His friend J.E. Snodgrass, who was a temperance advocate, claimed that Poe had fallen victim to a drinking binge. Snodgrass's account, along with that of Poe's attending physician, Dr. John Joseph Moran, who reported that Poe exhibited symptoms consistent with delirium tremens (a severe form of alcohol withdrawal), lend credence to the theory of death by alcohol abuse.

However, Dr. Moran's accounts of Poe's condition and death have been inconsistent and have varied significantly over time, casting doubt on their reliability. Furthermore, some of Poe's acquaintances, including his close friend Charles Baudelaire, argued that Poe had been sober in the months leading up to his death. This discrepancy has led some researchers to dismiss the alcoholism theory or consider it only as a contributing factor rather than the primary cause.

A less discussed but equally plausible theory is that Poe suffered from a medical condition that led to his death. Several potential conditions have been suggested, including diabetes, heart disease, epilepsy, and even rabies. In 1996, Dr. R. Michael Benitez, a cardiologist, published an article in the Maryland Medical Journal suggesting that Poe's symptoms were consistent with rabies. Rabies, a viral infection affecting the central nervous system, can cause agitation, confusion, and delirium, symptoms that matched Poe's presentation. While there is no direct evidence that Poe had rabies, this theory has gained some acceptance due to the symptomatic similarities.

Poe's mysterious final days have also led to speculation about poisoning. Some biographers and historians have suggested that Poe could have been intentionally poisoned, either by a malicious individual or through accidental exposure to toxins. Arsenic and mercury poisoning have both been considered as possible causes. During Poe's time, mercury was commonly used to treat various illnesses, including cholera, which Poe may have contracted during his travels. Chronic mercury poisoning can lead to symptoms such as confusion and hallucinations, which align with Poe's reported condition. However, there is no conclusive evidence to confirm this theory, and it remains speculative.

The possibility of foul play has also been explored. Poe had a number of personal and professional enemies, and some have speculated that he could have been murdered. One theory posits that Poe was targeted by the brothers of his fiancée, Sarah Elmira Royster, who disapproved of their engagement. Another suggests that he was killed by a literary rival or someone with a grudge against him. However, there is little concrete evidence to support these claims, and they remain largely in the realm of conjecture.

Complicating matters further are the inconsistencies in Dr. Moran's reports. Over the years, Moran provided varying accounts of Poe's final days, including differing descriptions of his symptoms, last words, and state of mind. These inconsistencies have made it difficult for historians to piece together a clear and accurate picture of Poe's death. Moran's reliability as a witness has been questioned, and his changing narratives have added layers of confusion to an already perplexing case.

In the absence of definitive evidence, the mystery of Edgar Allan Poe's death continues to invite speculation and debate. Each theory has its proponents and detractors, and the true cause of his demise may never be known. What is clear, however, is that Poe's life and death were marked by tragedy and hardship, elements that undoubtedly influenced his dark and haunting literary works. His untimely and enigmatic death has only added to his legend, cementing his place in American cultural and literary history.

Poe's legacy endures not only through his enduring works but also through the mystery of his death. His stories and poems, filled with themes of death, madness, and the supernatural, continue to captivate readers around the world. The unresolved nature of his death mirrors the unresolved tensions and questions in his writing, inviting readers to explore the boundaries of life, death, and the unknown.

The fascination with Poe's death has also led to numerous cultural references and adaptations. Books, films, and even theatrical productions have explored the mystery, each adding their own interpretations and theories. This ongoing interest ensures that Poe's story remains a subject of public intrigue and academic study.

In the end, the unresolved death of Edgar Allan Poe is a testament to the enduring power of mystery and the human desire for answers. It reflects the complexities of Poe's life and work, inviting endless speculation and exploration. As long as Poe's works continue to be read and appreciated, the mystery of his death will remain a compelling and integral part of his legacy, a haunting reminder of the enigmatic genius that shaped American literature.

Chapter 31: The Disappearance of Jimmy Hoffa

The disappearance of Jimmy Hoffa is one of the most enduring mysteries in American history, steeped in intrigue, organized crime, and speculation. James Riddle Hoffa, commonly known as Jimmy Hoffa, was a prominent labor union leader who played a pivotal role in the growth and development of the International Brotherhood of Teamsters (IBT), one of the largest and most powerful labor unions in the United States. Hoffa's rise to prominence in the 1950s and 1960s was marked by his charismatic leadership, his advocacy for workers' rights, and his deep involvement with organized crime, a combination that would eventually lead to his mysterious disappearance in 1975.

Hoffa was born on February 14, 1913, in Brazil, Indiana, into a working-class family. He began working at a young age and became involved in labor organizing in the 1930s. His skills as an organizer and negotiator quickly became apparent, and he rose through the ranks of the Teamsters. By 1957, he had become the national vice-president of the union and soon after, its president. Under Hoffa's leadership, the Teamsters grew significantly in power and influence, representing a vast network of truck drivers and other workers across the country. Hoffa was known for his strong-arm tactics, his ability to mobilize workers, and his willingness to confront employers and even the government to achieve better wages and working conditions for his members.

However, Hoffa's success was not without controversy. His tenure as a union leader was marred by allegations of corruption, mob connections, and criminal activities. The Teamsters under Hoffa became notorious for their connections with organized crime, with the union's pension fund being a particular point of interest. The fund, which held vast sums of money, was allegedly used to finance loans and investments in mafia-controlled businesses, including casinos in Las

Vegas. Hoffa's relationships with mafia figures were an open secret, and he often used these connections to solidify his control over the union and to intimidate rivals and adversaries.

Hoffa's criminal activities eventually caught the attention of the federal government, and he became the target of multiple investigations led by figures such as Robert F. Kennedy, who was then the Attorney General of the United States. Hoffa was convicted of jury tampering, attempted bribery, and fraud in 1967 and was sentenced to 13 years in prison. However, he maintained a significant degree of control over the Teamsters from behind bars and continued to be a powerful figure in the labor movement. In 1971, Hoffa was released from prison after receiving a commutation from President Richard Nixon, under the condition that he would not engage in union activities until 1980. This agreement, however, did little to diminish Hoffa's ambitions to regain his leadership position within the Teamsters.

Following his release, Hoffa actively sought to regain his influence in the union, despite the restrictions placed upon him. This pursuit led to increasing tensions with the new leadership of the Teamsters, particularly with Frank Fitzsimmons, who had succeeded Hoffa as president. Fitzsimmons was more amenable to the interests of organized crime, which preferred his less confrontational style of leadership compared to Hoffa's more aggressive approach. Hoffa's attempts to reassert his authority and his plans to expose corruption within the union reportedly angered various factions, including both union officials and organized crime figures who had benefited from the status quo.

The events leading up to Hoffa's disappearance are shrouded in mystery and speculation. On July 30, 1975, Hoffa was last seen outside the Machus Red Fox restaurant in Bloomfield Township, a suburb of Detroit, Michigan. He was reportedly there for a meeting with Anthony "Tony Jack" Giacalone, a Detroit mobster, and Anthony

"Tony Pro" Provenzano, a New Jersey Teamster official with known mafia ties. The nature of the meeting has been the subject of much conjecture, with some suggesting it was a negotiation for Hoffa's return to power, while others believe it was a setup for his elimination.

Hoffa's disappearance was immediately suspicious, as he was known to be punctual and responsible. When he failed to return home, his family reported him missing. An extensive search ensued, involving local and federal authorities, but no trace of Hoffa was ever found. His car was discovered in the restaurant's parking lot, but there was no sign of foul play or evidence to indicate what had happened to him. The case quickly became a media sensation, with widespread speculation about Hoffa's fate and the possible involvement of organized crime in his disappearance.

Over the years, numerous theories have emerged about what happened to Jimmy Hoffa. One popular theory is that he was murdered by mafia members who saw him as a threat to their control over the Teamsters and their lucrative interests tied to the union's pension fund. It is believed that Hoffa's body was disposed of in a manner that ensured it would never be found, with various accounts suggesting he was buried in a landfill, incinerated, or encased in concrete. Another theory posits that Hoffa was killed on orders from higher-ups within the union to prevent him from regaining power or exposing internal corruption.

The case has seen several high-profile investigations and searches for Hoffa's remains over the years, including digs at various sites across Michigan and New Jersey. These searches have been prompted by tips from informants, former mafia members, and Hoffa associates, but none have yielded conclusive evidence. The FBI and other law enforcement agencies have long suspected that Hoffa's disappearance was a result of a mob hit, but the lack of a body or definitive proof has made it one of the most famous unsolved mysteries in American history.

Hoffa was declared legally dead in 1982, but the intrigue surrounding his disappearance has persisted. The case has been the subject of numerous books, documentaries, and films, reflecting the public's enduring fascination with Hoffa's life and the circumstances of his disappearance. Theories about his fate continue to circulate, and the search for answers remains a topic of interest for both amateur sleuths and professional investigators.

The disappearance of Jimmy Hoffa not only underscores the risks associated with organized crime and union politics but also serves as a cautionary tale about the dangers of power and ambition. Hoffa's legacy as a labor leader is overshadowed by his criminal connections and the mystery of his disappearance, making him a complex and enigmatic figure in American history. His story is a poignant reminder of the dark underbelly of labor movements and the lengths to which individuals and organizations will go to maintain power and control.

Chapter 32: The Mysterious Death of George Reeves

The mysterious death of George Reeves, the actor best known for his role as Superman in the 1950s television series "Adventures of Superman," has been a subject of intrigue and speculation for decades. Born George Keefer Brewer on January 5, 1914, Reeves began his career in Hollywood in the late 1930s, eventually gaining fame as the iconic superhero. Despite his success on television, Reeves struggled with typecasting and dissatisfaction with his career trajectory, factors that some believe contributed to his untimely and controversial death on June 16, 1959.

George Reeves grew up in Pasadena, California, and pursued an acting career after attending Pasadena Junior College. He initially found success in minor film roles, including a part in the classic 1939 film "Gone with the Wind," where he played one of Scarlett O'Hara's suitors, Stuart Tarleton. However, Reeves's career didn't take off as expected, and he spent much of the 1940s in smaller roles and working in theater. It was in the early 1950s that he landed the role that would define his career and public persona: Superman.

"Adventures of Superman" premiered in 1952 and quickly became a popular show among children and families. Reeves's portrayal of Superman and his alter ego, Clark Kent, made him a household name. Despite the show's success and his newfound fame, Reeves reportedly struggled with being typecast in the role of the superhero. He found it difficult to secure roles in other genres, which led to professional frustration and concerns about his future in acting. Reeves also faced financial difficulties, as the show did not pay particularly well, and he was locked into a contract that limited his earnings and opportunities to take on other work.

These professional and financial pressures were compounded by personal issues. Reeves was engaged to Leonore Lemmon, a socialite with a reputation for a wild lifestyle. Their relationship was turbulent, and there were reports of arguments and discord. In addition to Lemmon, Reeves had a long-term relationship with Toni Mannix, the wife of MGM executive Eddie Mannix. Toni Mannix and Reeves had been involved for several years, and their relationship was widely known in Hollywood circles. The end of their affair and Reeves's engagement to Lemmon added another layer of complexity and tension to his personal life.

On the night of June 16, 1959, Reeves was found dead from a gunshot wound to the head in his home in the Benedict Canyon area of Los Angeles. The initial ruling by the police was that his death was a suicide. According to reports, Reeves had been out earlier in the evening with Lemmon and a few friends. After returning home, an argument allegedly ensued between Reeves and Lemmon. Witnesses claimed that Reeves, who was reportedly intoxicated, went upstairs, and shortly afterward, a gunshot was heard. Lemmon and the others present in the house claimed that they found Reeves lying on his bed with a gunshot wound to the head, a gun nearby.

The official ruling of suicide was met with skepticism and disbelief from some of Reeves's friends, family, and colleagues. They argued that Reeves was not the type to take his own life and that he had plans for the future, including potential new projects and a desire to direct. Questions arose about the circumstances of his death, particularly the behavior and statements of those present in the house that night. For instance, some reports indicated that it took a significant amount of time before anyone called the police, and there were inconsistencies in the accounts of what happened in the moments leading up to and following the shooting.

One theory that emerged was that Reeves's death was not a suicide but rather a homicide, possibly linked to his relationships with Leonore

Lemmon and Toni Mannix. Some speculated that Lemmon, who had a volatile relationship with Reeves, might have been involved in his death, either accidentally or intentionally. Others pointed to the Mannix family, suggesting that Eddie Mannix, known for his connections to organized crime and reputation for handling scandals discreetly, might have been involved due to jealousy or to prevent a potential scandal involving his wife Toni and Reeves. However, no conclusive evidence was ever found to support these theories.

Another point of contention was the physical evidence. There were reports of bruises on Reeves's body, which some interpreted as signs of a struggle, though these could have been the result of his physical activities or an unrelated incident. Additionally, the positioning of the gun and the trajectory of the bullet raised questions. Some believed that the angle of the shot was unusual for a self-inflicted wound, suggesting that someone else might have been involved.

The coroner's report ultimately upheld the initial suicide ruling, but the inconsistencies and unanswered questions fueled ongoing speculation and conspiracy theories. The case was closed, and Reeves was buried, but the mystery surrounding his death continued to capture public interest. The lack of a definitive resolution led to numerous books, documentaries, and articles exploring various theories about what might have happened. The story was further popularized by the 2006 film "Hollywoodland," which dramatized the events leading up to Reeves's death and examined the different possibilities surrounding it.

George Reeves's death remains one of Hollywood's most enduring mysteries. The combination of his iconic role as Superman, the murky circumstances of his death, and the involvement of notable Hollywood figures and alleged connections to organized crime create a story that continues to fascinate and perplex. Whether Reeves's death was a tragic suicide, a murder, or an accidental shooting, the lack of concrete answers ensures that his final moments are the subject of ongoing debate and speculation.

The case highlights the pressures and pitfalls of Hollywood fame, particularly for actors who become closely identified with a single role. Reeves's struggle with typecasting and his efforts to transition to other parts of the entertainment industry reflect broader challenges faced by many actors. Additionally, the potential involvement of influential figures and the rumors of mob connections underscore the sometimes-hidden complexities and dangers of life in the entertainment world.

In the end, the mysterious death of George Reeves serves as a cautionary tale about the darker side of fame and the unresolved questions that can linger long after the public spotlight has faded. His legacy as Superman endures, but so does the intrigue surrounding the final chapter of his life, a puzzle that continues to captivate and confound those who seek to uncover the truth.

Chapter 33: The Case of D. B. Cooper

The case of D. B. Cooper is one of the most enduring and intriguing mysteries in American criminal history. It involves the hijacking of a Boeing 727 aircraft in 1971 by a man who used the alias "Dan Cooper," later mistakenly identified by the media as "D. B. Cooper." This individual parachuted out of the plane with a ransom of $200,000 and was never seen again, sparking decades of investigation, speculation, and folklore.

On the afternoon of November 24, 1971, a man identifying himself as Dan Cooper purchased a one-way ticket from Portland, Oregon, to Seattle, Washington, on Northwest Orient Airlines Flight 305. Described as a middle-aged man in his mid-40s, Cooper was dressed in a business suit with a black tie and white shirt, and he carried a black attaché case. Once aboard the aircraft, Cooper handed a note to a flight attendant, Florence Schaffner, indicating that he had a bomb. Initially dismissing the note as a flirtatious overture, Schaffner did not immediately respond. However, when Cooper reiterated his threat, Schaffner read the note, which stated that he had a bomb and instructed her to sit next to him. He then showed her the contents of his briefcase, which appeared to contain a bomb with wires, red sticks, and a battery.

Cooper demanded $200,000 in "negotiable American currency," four parachutes (two primary and two reserve), and a fuel truck standing by in Seattle to refuel the aircraft upon landing. Schaffner conveyed Cooper's demands to the cockpit, and the pilot informed air traffic control, leading to the involvement of the FBI. The airline agreed to meet Cooper's demands, and the plane circled Puget Sound for about two hours to allow authorities time to gather the ransom money and parachutes. During this time, Cooper exhibited calm and polite behavior, even ordering a bourbon and soda and offering to pay for his drink.

Upon landing at Seattle-Tacoma International Airport, Cooper allowed the 36 passengers and some of the flight attendants to disembark in exchange for the ransom money and parachutes, which were delivered to the plane. He kept several crew members, including the pilot, co-pilot, and a flight attendant, onboard. After the refueling was completed, Cooper outlined his flight plan to the cockpit crew, specifying a course toward Mexico City at a low altitude of 10,000 feet and a speed of 150 knots. He also requested that the landing gear remain deployed in the takeoff position and that the cabin remain unpressurized.

Cooper's precise knowledge of the aircraft's technical specifications and flight capabilities suggested that he had some background in aviation, either as a pilot, a crew member, or through military experience. As the aircraft took off from Seattle, Cooper instructed the remaining flight attendant to join the rest of the crew in the cockpit and remain there with the door closed. At approximately 8:00 p.m., as the plane flew over the rugged terrain of southwestern Washington, Cooper lowered the aircraft's rear stairs and jumped into the night, taking the ransom money with him. This was the last confirmed sighting of Cooper, who vanished into the stormy night sky.

The FBI, in conjunction with local law enforcement, launched an extensive manhunt to locate Cooper, but no trace of him was found. The search area, based on flight path estimates, covered a vast and remote region of forested land, making the task of finding Cooper or any evidence exceptionally challenging. The case was further complicated by the lack of precise information on Cooper's landing zone due to uncertainties about the plane's exact speed and the wind conditions at the time of the jump.

In the months and years following the hijacking, the FBI conducted numerous interviews and pursued various leads, but none resulted in Cooper's identification or capture. The agency released sketches of Cooper based on descriptions provided by the flight crew and passengers, and thousands of tips were investigated. Despite these efforts, Cooper's true identity and fate remained a mystery. Some speculated that Cooper had not survived the jump, given the harsh weather conditions and the difficulty of parachuting into a densely forested area at night without proper equipment or preparation. Others believed he had successfully escaped and disappeared.

The case gained new life in 1980 when an eight-year-old boy named Brian Ingram discovered a decaying package containing $5,800 in $20 bills along the Columbia River, about 20 miles southwest of Cooper's estimated drop zone. The serial numbers on the bills matched those of the ransom money, confirming that the money was indeed part of the hijacking loot. This discovery, known as the "Tina Bar find," provided a significant clue but also raised more questions. It was unclear how the money ended up in the river, whether Cooper had deliberately buried it or lost it during the jump, or if it had drifted there over time. The condition of the bills suggested they had been in the elements for some time, but forensic analysis provided no conclusive answers.

The FBI continued to investigate the case for decades, following numerous theories and potential leads. One line of inquiry involved suspects who had either a background in aviation or military service, given Cooper's apparent knowledge of aircraft and parachuting. Some suspects emerged from criminal backgrounds or were involved in similar hijackings or crimes. However, none of these leads produced definitive evidence linking any individual to the crime.

In July 2016, the FBI formally closed the active investigation into the D. B. Cooper case, citing the need to allocate resources to more pressing concerns. The case, however, remains officially open, and any significant evidence or credible leads could prompt a renewed investigation. The closing of the case without resolution has left a significant void in the narrative, prompting continued public fascination and amateur sleuthing.

Several theories have been proposed over the years regarding Cooper's identity and fate. Some speculate that Cooper was an experienced skydiver or former paratrooper who had the skills necessary to survive the jump and evade capture. Others suggest that he perished in the wilderness, with his body and the remaining ransom money still undiscovered. There are also theories that Cooper had an accomplice who helped him escape, possibly by meeting him on the ground or in another aircraft.

The D. B. Cooper case has become a cultural phenomenon, inspiring books, documentaries, films, and countless amateur investigations. The figure of Cooper, often romanticized as a folk hero or modern-day Robin Hood, represents a fascinating enigma in American criminal history. The case continues to captivate the public imagination, embodying themes of mystery, adventure, and the allure of the unknown.

The enduring mystery of D. B. Cooper is not just about the crime itself but also about the questions it raises about identity, justice, and the capacity for one person to vanish without a trace in the modern world. Cooper's ability to execute such a bold and well-planned heist, coupled with the complete absence of any concrete evidence regarding his fate, challenges our assumptions about law enforcement's capabilities and the boundaries of human ingenuity. The case remains a quintessential example of an unsolved mystery that resists resolution, inviting speculation, debate, and the enduring hope that one day, the truth will be revealed.

Chapter 34: The Long Island Serial Killer

The Long Island Serial Killer, also known as the Gilgo Beach Killer, is a mysterious and unidentified individual or possibly individuals believed to be responsible for the murders of at least 10 to 16 people, mostly women, whose remains have been discovered in and around the Gilgo Beach area on Long Island, New York. This case is one of the most perplexing and high-profile unsolved serial murder investigations in the United States, drawing widespread attention and speculation due to the brutality of the crimes, the challenges faced by law enforcement in identifying the perpetrator, and the complex web of potential victims and suspects involved.

The case came to public attention in December 2010, when the Suffolk County Police Department was conducting a training exercise involving a K-9 unit along the Ocean Parkway near Gilgo Beach. During this exercise, a cadaver dog discovered the skeletal remains of a woman wrapped in burlap. This discovery led to a larger search of the area, resulting in the unearthing of more bodies. Over the following months, additional remains were found, scattered along a stretch of highway on the south shore of Long Island. The victims were predominantly young women who had been involved in sex work, although the identities and backgrounds of all the victims vary.

The identification of the victims has been a challenging aspect of the investigation. Initially, the first four sets of remains found in December 2010 were identified as Maureen Brainard-Barnes, Melissa Barthelemy, Megan Waterman, and Amber Lynn Costello. These women were all known to have advertised their services on Craigslist, a platform frequently used by sex workers at the time. The discovery of their remains suggested that the killer may have targeted individuals working in the sex trade, exploiting their vulnerability and the relative anonymity of their occupation. The similarities in the victims' lifestyles and the circumstances of their disappearances provided investigators with initial clues, but they also highlighted the difficulties in tracing their movements and contacts.

In 2011, the search expanded and led to the discovery of additional remains, including partial skeletal remains that had been found previously at other locations on Long Island. Among these were the remains of Jessica Taylor, whose torso had been found in Manorville, New York, in 2003, and a yet-unidentified woman known as "Peaches," whose torso was discovered in Hempstead Lake State Park in 1997. The linking of these cases suggested that the killer or killers had been active for many years and possibly used multiple sites for disposing of bodies.

One of the most disturbing aspects of the case is the apparent method of disposal and the condition in which some of the bodies were found. Several victims were dismembered, and their remains scattered across different locations. This pattern of dismemberment and dispersal complicates the process of identifying victims and understanding the timeline of the murders. Additionally, the use of burlap to wrap some of the bodies indicates a degree of premeditation and an effort to prevent or delay discovery.

The complexity of the case has been compounded by the discovery of remains that do not fit neatly into a single profile or timeline. For example, the skeletal remains of a toddler and an Asian male were also found during the investigation. The toddler, believed to be the daughter of "Peaches," was found near her mother's remains, while the Asian male, who was dressed in women's clothing, was discovered separately. The presence of these victims raises questions about the killer's motives and whether there might be multiple perpetrators with differing victim profiles or if a single individual is responsible for a wider range of crimes than initially suspected.

Over the years, the investigation has faced numerous challenges, including jurisdictional issues between different law enforcement agencies, the potential involvement of multiple perpetrators, and the transient and often vulnerable nature of the victims' lives, which makes tracing their last movements difficult. The Suffolk County Police Department, the FBI, and other agencies have been involved in the investigation, but the case remains unsolved. The release of limited information to the public and occasional disputes between agencies have also contributed to speculation and criticism regarding the handling of the case.

One aspect of the case that has generated significant controversy is the role of former Suffolk County Police Chief James Burke. Burke was later convicted of assault and obstruction of justice in an unrelated case, which raised concerns about the integrity of the investigation under his leadership. There were allegations that Burke may have hindered FBI involvement in the investigation to prevent scrutiny of his own actions and those of his department. These developments cast a shadow over the investigation and fueled conspiracy theories about potential cover-ups or corruption.

Despite the challenges, there have been some investigative efforts that have provided new leads. For example, in 2011, police released a composite sketch of an unidentified victim, known as "Jane Doe No. 6," whose partial remains were found both in Manorville and along Ocean Parkway. Advances in forensic technology, including DNA analysis and forensic genealogy, have also offered new avenues for identifying victims and potential suspects. However, these efforts have yet to yield a definitive break in the case.

Public interest in the case has been sustained over the years by media coverage, documentaries, and books, which have explored various aspects of the investigation, potential suspects, and the lives of the victims. This attention has kept the case in the public eye and generated widespread speculation about the identity of the killer or killers. Several individuals have been considered persons of interest or suspects over the years, including convicted criminals and individuals known to frequent the areas where the victims were last seen. However, none of these individuals have been conclusively linked to the murders.

The Long Island Serial Killer case remains an active investigation, with law enforcement agencies continuing to pursue leads and examine evidence. The Suffolk County Police Department has periodically released information to the public in the hopes of generating new tips or leads. In January 2020, they released images of a belt with distinctive initials, believed to belong to the killer, in an attempt to solicit public assistance in identifying the owner.

The enduring mystery of the Long Island Serial Killer highlights the challenges faced in investigating serial crimes, particularly those involving marginalized victims such as sex workers. The case underscores the importance of interagency cooperation, the need for public engagement, and the potential of forensic advancements in solving long-standing criminal cases. As of now, the killer or killers remain unidentified, and the families of the victims continue to seek answers and justice for their loved ones. The case remains one of the most notorious and haunting unsolved mysteries in the history of American crime.

Chapter 35: The Green Bicycle Mystery

The Green Bicycle Mystery, also known as the Green Bicycle Case, revolves around the unsolved murder of Bella Wright, a young woman found dead on a rural road in Leicestershire, England, in 1919. The case is named after the green bicycle that played a central role in the investigation, becoming a symbol of the intrigue and unanswered questions that have surrounded the crime for over a century.

Bella Wright, born Ann Isabella Wright on July 31, 1897, was the daughter of an agricultural laborer. She lived in the village of Stoughton, near Leicester, and worked in a factory. On July 5, 1919, Bella Wright was last seen alive cycling on her way to visit her uncle, George Measures, in the nearby village of Gaulby. At around 6:30 p.m., she arrived at her uncle's home, where they had a brief conversation. During this visit, a man on a green bicycle was noticed waiting outside. Bella told her uncle that the man was a stranger who had offered her assistance with a mechanical issue on her bicycle earlier that day. This man was described as being of medium build, clean-shaven, and well-dressed.

After leaving her uncle's house, Bella and the man on the green bicycle were seen cycling together. The two were observed by several witnesses along the route they took, heading towards the village of Little Stretton. At approximately 9:30 p.m., Bella Wright was found dead by a farmer named Joseph Cowell on a quiet road known as Gartree Road, near the village of Little Stretton. Her bicycle lay on the ground nearby, and she had suffered a gunshot wound to the head. The position of her body and the condition of the scene initially led Cowell and others who arrived at the scene to believe that she had suffered a cycling accident, but upon closer examination, it became clear that she had been shot.

The discovery of Bella Wright's body and the circumstances of her death sparked immediate concern and speculation. The investigation, led by Detective Chief Inspector Robert Collett of the Leicester City Police, focused on identifying the man on the green bicycle seen with her earlier that evening. The search for this individual became the focal point of the inquiry, as it was presumed he could either be the killer or a key witness.

The case quickly gained media attention, with the green bicycle becoming a central element in the reporting and public imagination. The description of the man and the bicycle was widely circulated, and a large-scale search was conducted to locate both. The authorities also checked bicycle shops and repair establishments for any information about recent purchases or repairs that might match the description of the green bicycle. However, despite these efforts, the man and the bicycle remained elusive.

As the investigation progressed, several pieces of evidence emerged, including a bullet and spent cartridge case found at the scene, which indicated that Bella had been shot with a .455-caliber revolver. Despite this, the investigation faced significant challenges. The lack of witnesses to the actual crime, the rural and isolated location, and the minimal physical evidence available made it difficult to establish a clear narrative of what had happened.

The breakthrough in the case came several weeks later, on July 23, 1919, when a green bicycle matching the description was found in a local canal by two boys. The bicycle was retrieved and examined, revealing that it had been deliberately stripped of identifying marks and dumped. This discovery reinvigorated the investigation, as it suggested that the man with the green bicycle had attempted to conceal his identity and his connection to the crime. Further inquiries led the police to Ronald Light, a 34-year-old former soldier and schoolteacher living in Leicester. Light was known to own a green bicycle and matched the description of the man seen with Bella Wright.

Ronald Light was arrested on March 4, 1920, and charged with Bella Wright's murder. His trial took place at Leicester Assizes in June

1920 and attracted significant public interest. The prosecution's case centered on circumstantial evidence, including the identification of the bicycle and witnesses who had seen Light with Bella. Additionally, a bullet of the same caliber as the one found at the scene was discovered in Light's possession, and he had a history of odd behavior and military experience, which the prosecution suggested made him capable of committing the crime.

Light's defense, led by renowned barrister Sir Edward Marshall Hall, argued that while Light had indeed been with Bella Wright on the day of her death, he was not responsible for her murder. Light claimed that after parting ways with Bella, he continued on his own and was unaware of her fate until he read about it in the newspapers. The defense also questioned the reliability of the witnesses and pointed out that there was no direct evidence linking Light to the murder, such as the gun used in the crime or any forensic evidence.

The trial culminated in a dramatic and unexpected outcome. Despite the prosecution's case and the suspicious circumstances surrounding Light's behavior, the jury acquitted him of all charges. The decision hinged on the lack of direct evidence and the persuasive arguments of the defense, which successfully cast doubt on Light's guilt. Ronald Light was freed, and the case officially remained unsolved.

The acquittal of Ronald Light did not put an end to the speculation and debate surrounding the Green Bicycle Mystery. The case has continued to intrigue and puzzle investigators, historians, and the public alike. Over the years, various theories and interpretations have emerged, ranging from the possibility of a botched robbery or assault to more elaborate suggestions involving secret lovers or conspiracies. Some have speculated that Light was indeed the killer but that the evidence was insufficient to prove his guilt beyond a reasonable doubt. Others have suggested that another unknown individual was responsible, possibly taking advantage of the situation to commit the crime and frame Light.

The Green Bicycle Mystery remains one of the most famous unsolved cases in British criminal history. It highlights the challenges of early 20th-century forensic and investigative techniques, where reliance on eyewitness testimony and circumstantial evidence often made or broke a case. The case also serves as a fascinating study in the influence of public perception, media coverage, and courtroom strategy on the outcome of criminal trials.

In recent years, renewed interest in the case has led to further investigations and discussions, including books and documentaries exploring the known facts and theories. Despite these efforts, the identity of Bella Wright's killer remains unknown, and the green bicycle continues to symbolize the enigmatic and unresolved nature of the crime. The mystery endures as a haunting reminder of how justice, truth, and memory can be elusive, and how some stories, despite the passage of time and the advances in technology, may never be fully understood or resolved.

Chapter 36: The Lake Bodom Murders

The Lake Bodom Murders, one of Finland's most infamous and enduring criminal mysteries, occurred on the night of June 4-5, 1960, near the town of Espoo, close to Helsinki. The case involves the brutal killing of three teenagers and the severe injury of a fourth while they were camping on the shores of Lake Bodom. Despite extensive investigations over the decades, the case remains unsolved, shrouded in speculation, conflicting evidence, and a series of suspects who have come under scrutiny without any conclusive resolution.

The victims were four Finnish teenagers: Anja Tuulikki Mäki, 15, Maila Irmeli Björklund, 15, Seppo Antero Boisman, 18, and Nils Wilhelm Gustafsson, 18. They had set up camp on the evening of June 4, 1960, planning to spend a peaceful night by the lake. Sometime during the night or early morning hours, an unknown assailant attacked the group, stabbing and bludgeoning them with a sharp object and a blunt instrument, possibly a rock or a pipe. The attack was savage and seemingly random, leaving three of the teenagers dead and one, Nils Gustafsson, severely injured but alive.

The bodies of Anja Mäki and Seppo Boisman were found inside the collapsed tent, while Irmeli Björklund's body was discovered on top of the tent, suggesting she had been dragged out during the attack. Nils Gustafsson was found outside the tent with severe injuries, including a fractured jaw and facial bruises. Remarkably, despite his injuries, Gustafsson survived, though he had no recollection of the attack when he was discovered.

The discovery of the crime scene was made by a group of boys birdwatching nearby, who noticed the collapsed tent and the lifeless bodies. They alerted authorities, sparking a massive investigation led by the Finnish police. The crime scene presented a perplexing array of evidence and unanswered questions. The victims' shoes were missing and later found some distance from the tent, along with various other personal belongings scattered around the area. The disarray and brutality of the scene suggested a sudden and frenzied attack, yet there were no clear signs of a motive, such as theft or sexual assault.

The investigation faced numerous challenges from the outset. The police were criticized for their handling of the crime scene, as they allowed numerous officers and onlookers to trample the area, potentially contaminating or destroying crucial evidence. Additionally, forensic techniques at the time were not as advanced as they are today, limiting the ability to gather definitive physical evidence. The lack of clear fingerprints, DNA evidence, or other forensic markers complicated the identification of the perpetrator.

Initial theories about the crime ranged widely, from a random act of violence by a transient or a mentally disturbed individual to the possibility of a more personal motive involving the victims. The area around Lake Bodom was scoured for evidence, and extensive interviews were conducted with locals and anyone who might have been in the vicinity. However, the investigation struggled to yield solid leads, and public anxiety grew as the lack of an arrest or clear suspect became apparent.

Over the years, several individuals came under suspicion, and the case saw various developments and twists. One early suspect was a local kiosk keeper named Väinö "Väiski" Viitanen, who had been seen in the area on the night of the murders. Viitanen had a history of minor offenses and was known for his erratic behavior, but there was no direct evidence linking him to the crime, and he was eventually released after questioning.

Another theory that gained attention was the possibility that the murders were the work of a foreigner, possibly a German, given that the crime occurred during a period when Finland was experiencing an influx of visitors from abroad. This theory was partly fueled by the discovery of unusual footprints at the scene and the fact that the murder weapon was never found, suggesting it might have been disposed of by someone unfamiliar with the area. However, this line of inquiry also failed to produce concrete results.

The case took a surprising turn in 2004 when, after more than 40 years, Nils Gustafsson, the sole survivor, was arrested and charged with the murders of his friends. This arrest was based on new forensic evidence and a re-examination of the case, including the positioning of the bodies and the nature of Gustafsson's injuries. The prosecution argued that Gustafsson, in a drunken rage possibly triggered by jealousy or a fight with his friends, had committed the murders. They pointed to the fact that Gustafsson's injuries, while severe, were less life-threatening than those sustained by the other victims, suggesting a potential self-inflicted or staged nature.

Gustafsson's trial in 2005 was a media sensation in Finland, drawing significant public interest and debate. The defense argued that Gustafsson had no motive to kill his friends and highlighted inconsistencies in the prosecution's case, including the fact that no murder weapon was ever found and that the forensic evidence was circumstantial. They also questioned the reliability of memories and witness statements given the passage of time and changes in forensic technology and understanding.

Ultimately, the jury acquitted Gustafsson of all charges, citing insufficient evidence to convict him beyond a reasonable doubt. The acquittal did little to dispel the cloud of mystery surrounding the case, as many in the public and media continued to speculate about Gustafsson's possible involvement, while others criticized the police and judicial system for not finding the true culprit.

The Lake Bodom Murders remain a deeply troubling cold case, marked by a combination of sensationalism, speculation, and the frustrations of an investigation that has spanned decades without resolution. The case has inspired books, documentaries, and even a feature film, each exploring different theories and aspects of the crime. The enduring fascination with the case is partly due to the brutal nature of the murders, the youth of the victims, and the picturesque setting of Lake Bodom, which contrasts starkly with the horror of the events that unfolded there.

In recent years, advances in forensic science, particularly in DNA analysis, have renewed hope among some that the case might eventually be solved. However, the degradation of evidence over time and the initial mishandling of the crime scene present significant obstacles. The case remains officially open, and the Finnish police occasionally revisit the evidence in light of new technologies or information, but as of now, no definitive answers have emerged.

The Lake Bodom Murders serve as a stark reminder of the limitations of criminal investigations, particularly in an era before modern forensic methods, and the profound impact such crimes have on the victims' families, the community, and the collective consciousness. The mystery of who killed Anja Mäki, Maila Björklund, and Seppo Boisman, and why, continues to haunt the Finnish psyche, leaving a legacy of unanswered questions and a chilling narrative that has become part of Finland's criminal folklore.

Chapter 37: The Murder of Martha Moxley

The murder of Martha Moxley is one of the most notorious unsolved crimes in American history, both for its brutality and for the high-profile nature of the individuals involved. The case has captivated public attention for decades due to its connections to the wealthy and influential Kennedy family, the prolonged legal battles, and the persistent mystery surrounding the circumstances of the crime. The events unfolded in the affluent community of Belle Haven, Greenwich, Connecticut, and involved the violent death of a 15-year-old girl named Martha Moxley on the night of October 30, 1975, a date known locally as "Mischief Night," traditionally a time of pranks and minor vandalism.

Martha Moxley was a popular and well-liked teenager, described as friendly, outgoing, and active in her school and community. She lived with her family in the upscale neighborhood of Belle Haven, a gated enclave known for its opulent homes and prominent residents. On the evening of October 30, Martha went out with friends, planning to engage in the typical teenage mischief associated with the night before Halloween. The group ended up at the home of the Skakel family, who lived nearby. The Skakels were a prominent family, related to the Kennedy clan through Ethel Skakel, who was married to Robert F. Kennedy.

The Skakel household was known for its large size and the frequent absence of parental supervision, as the Skakel children were raised primarily by tutors and house staff after their mother's death and their father's frequent travels. The two eldest Skakel brothers, Thomas (Tommy) and Michael, were both known to Martha and her friends. According to witness accounts, Martha was last seen around 9:30 p.m. with Tommy Skakel near the Skakel home. The events that transpired after that time remain unclear and are the subject of much debate and speculation.

Martha did not return home that night, and her mother, Dorthy Moxley, reported her missing the next morning. A search of the neighborhood ensued, and tragically, Martha's body was discovered under a tree on her family's property. She had been brutally attacked, with multiple blunt force trauma injuries to her head, inflicted by a golf club, which was found broken into pieces near her body. An autopsy later revealed that Martha had also been stabbed in the neck with a piece of the club's broken shaft. The ferocity of the attack and the use of a golf club, an unusual weapon, shocked the community and led to widespread speculation about the identity of the killer and their motive.

The initial investigation into Martha's murder faced several challenges. The Greenwich Police Department, unaccustomed to handling such violent crimes, struggled with the case's complexity and the intense media scrutiny it attracted. The case quickly became a national sensation, partly due to the Skakel family's connection to the Kennedys and the privileged nature of the community. This high-profile nature led to accusations of a botched investigation, with critics alleging that the Skakel family's influence had hindered the police's efforts to investigate thoroughly.

Early in the investigation, Tommy Skakel emerged as a person of interest. He admitted to being with Martha on the night of her murder but provided inconsistent accounts of their interactions. Initially, Tommy claimed that he and Martha had parted ways around 9:30 p.m., and he had then gone to his room to do schoolwork. However, his story changed during subsequent interviews, leading to suspicion and speculation about his potential involvement. Despite these inconsistencies, no charges were filed against Tommy or anyone else in the immediate aftermath, and the case went cold.

Over the years, the Moxley murder case saw numerous developments, as new evidence, theories, and suspects emerged. One significant turn in the investigation occurred in the late 1990s when journalist and author Mark Fuhrman, a former Los Angeles police detective, published a book titled "Murder in Greenwich." Fuhrman, who had gained national attention during the O.J. Simpson trial, presented a detailed examination of the case, suggesting that Michael Skakel, rather than Tommy, was the prime suspect. Fuhrman argued that Michael, who was 15 at the time of the murder, had been infatuated with Martha and might have killed her in a jealous rage after seeing her with Tommy.

This theory was bolstered by Michael Skakel's own erratic behavior and changing alibis over the years. Initially, Michael claimed to have been at a cousin's house watching television at the time of the murder, but later admitted to having returned to the Moxley property that night to climb a tree and peep into Martha's window. Furthermore, several people who had attended a substance abuse treatment center with Michael years after the murder came forward, claiming he had made incriminating statements about the case.

In 2000, a grand jury was convened to investigate the murder further, leading to Michael Skakel's arrest and indictment for Martha Moxley's murder. The arrest marked a significant breakthrough in a case that had long seemed destined to remain unsolved. The trial, held in 2002, drew extensive media coverage, with the prosecution painting a picture of a troubled and angry young man who had lashed out violently when spurned by Martha. They presented evidence, including witness testimonies and Michael's own contradictory statements, to support the theory that he had killed Martha with a golf club taken from the Skakel home.

The defense argued that the evidence against Michael was circumstantial and that the passage of time had compromised the reliability of witness statements and memories. They also suggested alternative suspects, including Kenneth Littleton, a former live-in tutor for the Skakel family, who had been present in the household at the time of the murder and had exhibited suspicious behavior afterward. However, the jury found Michael Skakel guilty of murder, and he was sentenced to 20 years to life in prison.

The conviction, however, did not bring a final resolution to the case. Michael Skakel maintained his innocence, and his legal team continued to fight for his release, arguing that his trial had been unfair and that he had been wrongfully convicted. They pointed to issues such as inadequate representation, unreliable witnesses, and the failure to consider potentially exculpatory evidence. In 2013, a judge granted Skakel a new trial, citing ineffective counsel during his original trial, and ordered his release on bail. The decision was later upheld, and in 2018, the Connecticut Supreme Court vacated Skakel's conviction, ruling that his right to a fair trial had been violated.

As of now, the legal status of the case remains in a state of flux, with ongoing appeals and legal maneuvers. The vacating of Skakel's conviction does not equate to a declaration of innocence, but rather a recognition of procedural flaws in the original trial. The state has the option to retry Skakel, but the likelihood of a new trial diminishes as time passes and memories fade, complicating the pursuit of justice.

The murder of Martha Moxley continues to be a source of fascination and frustration for those seeking closure. The case has been the subject of numerous books, documentaries, and television specials, each offering different perspectives and theories. The involvement of the Skakel family and their connection to the Kennedys has added a layer of intrigue and conspiracy theories, with some suggesting that powerful forces may have influenced the course of the investigation and the trial.

At the heart of the case remains the tragic and senseless death of a young girl whose life was brutally cut short. For Martha Moxley's family, the quest for justice has been a long and painful journey, marked by moments of hope and disappointment. The community of Greenwich, too, has been indelibly affected by the case, which shattered the image of tranquility and safety that often accompanies affluent suburban areas.

The Martha Moxley case serves as a poignant reminder of the complexities and challenges of the criminal justice system, particularly in high-profile cases involving wealth and social connections. It highlights the difficulties in achieving a clear and definitive resolution in legal proceedings, where the passage of time, the fallibility of memory, and the intricacies of the law can all play crucial roles.

As of now, the question of who killed Martha Moxley remains officially unresolved, leaving a lingering sense of uncertainty and injustice. The case stands as a testament to the enduring impact of violent crime on individuals, families, and communities, and the persistent hope that one day, the truth may be fully uncovered and justice served.

Chapter 38: The Circleville Letters Mystery

The Circleville Letters Mystery is a perplexing case that centers around an anonymous writer who terrorized the small town of Circleville, Ohio, with a series of threatening letters. The saga, which began in 1976, involves accusations of infidelity, corruption, and criminal behavior, leading to an attempted murder, a suspicious death, and a controversial legal battle. The case remains unresolved, shrouded in mystery and speculation, and has become a notable example of the impact of anonymous communication and psychological intimidation in a close-knit community.

The strange events in Circleville, a rural town located about 25 miles south of Columbus, began when residents started receiving letters filled with disturbing and intimate details about their private lives. These letters, which were postmarked from nearby Columbus, accused recipients of various misdeeds, from infidelity and theft to allegations of illegal activities. The letters were written in block letters to disguise the writer's handwriting and often contained explicit threats. The most prominent target of these letters was Mary Gillespie, a local school bus driver.

Mary Gillespie received the first of many letters in March 1977. The letter accused her of having an affair with Gordon Massie, the superintendent of the Westfall School District, where she worked. The letter demanded that she end the alleged affair or face public exposure. Mary denied the allegations, but the letters continued, increasing in frequency and severity. They were addressed to Mary, her husband Ron, and other individuals in the community, often containing explicit language and threats of violence. The letters also contained details about the lives of the recipients, suggesting that the writer was someone familiar with the town and its residents.

Despite the menacing nature of the letters, the Gillespies attempted to keep the matter private, confiding only in close family and friends. However, the situation escalated dramatically on August 19, 1977. That evening, Ron Gillespie received a phone call that reportedly upset him. He left the house in a hurry, taking his gun with him, and told his children he was going to confront the letter writer. Ron was found dead shortly afterward, in his crashed pickup truck, having apparently lost control of the vehicle and hit a tree. Strangely, his gun had been fired once, but the bullet was not found. The official investigation ruled Ron's death an accident caused by alcohol impairment, despite his family insisting that he had not been drinking that day. This ruling was controversial, given the threatening letters and the suspicious circumstances surrounding Ron's death.

Following Ron's death, the letter writer continued to send messages, now accusing Mary of being responsible for her husband's demise. These new letters suggested that Ron's death was not an accident, further stoking fears and suspicions within the community. The writer even began posting signs along Mary's bus route, making lurid claims about her and others. In a particularly chilling development, these signs sometimes included booby-trapped boxes designed to harm anyone who attempted to remove them. In February 1983, Mary spotted one such sign and stopped to remove it. She discovered a box attached to a crude device intended to fire a gun upon opening. The gun was found to belong to Paul Freshour, Mary's brother-in-law, who was then arrested and charged with attempted murder.

Paul Freshour denied any involvement in the letters or the booby trap. However, during the investigation, it was revealed that Freshour had separated from his wife, Ron Gillespie's sister, who accused him of writing the letters. Freshour was put on trial for attempted murder in 1983, where prosecutors presented evidence linking him to the booby trap. Notably, handwriting experts testified that Freshour's writing matched samples from the letters, despite the block-style lettering meant to disguise the author's handwriting. The defense argued that the evidence was circumstantial and that the handwriting analysis was flawed. Nevertheless, Freshour was found guilty of attempted murder and sentenced to 7 to 25 years in prison. Interestingly, during his incarceration, the letters continued to be sent, not only to Mary but also to other residents, as well as to officials involved in the case.

The continuation of the letters while Freshour was in prison cast doubt on his guilt in the public's eyes. He consistently maintained his innocence, suggesting that he had been framed and that the real letter writer was still at large. The letters persisted for several years, even reaching media outlets and demanding that the case be reopened and Freshour exonerated. These developments led to widespread speculation about the true identity of the letter writer, with theories ranging from a complex conspiracy involving multiple individuals to the possibility of an outsider with detailed knowledge of the town's affairs.

Freshour's case gained renewed attention when the television show "Unsolved Mysteries" featured it in 1994. The program highlighted the inconsistencies and unanswered questions surrounding the investigation and trial, such as the lack of physical evidence directly linking Freshour to the letters or the booby trap. Additionally, "Unsolved Mysteries" revealed that Freshour had passed a polygraph test, which had not been considered during his trial. Despite these revelations and ongoing public interest, Freshour's conviction was not overturned, and he served ten years in prison before being released on parole in 1994. He continued to assert his innocence until his death in 2012.

The Circleville Letters Mystery remains an unsolved case, with no definitive answers about the true identity of the letter writer or the motivations behind the campaign of harassment. The case has sparked numerous theories, some suggesting that the letters were part of a coordinated effort to target and discredit specific individuals, while others propose that the letter writer acted alone, possibly driven by personal grievances or psychological issues. The mystery has also raised questions about the effectiveness of the criminal justice system in handling cases involving anonymous threats and psychological intimidation.

In recent years, advances in forensic science, particularly in the analysis of handwriting and forensic linguistics, have opened new avenues for potentially resolving the case. However, the original letters and evidence would need to be re-examined using these modern techniques, a prospect complicated by the passage of time and potential degradation of materials. The case continues to be a topic of fascination for true crime enthusiasts, journalists, and researchers, who are drawn to its enigmatic nature and the enduring question of who was behind the Circleville letters and why they chose to terrorize this small Ohio town.

The Circleville Letters Mystery serves as a stark reminder of the power of anonymous communication and the profound impact it can have on individuals and communities. The case highlights the challenges faced by law enforcement in investigating crimes that lack clear physical evidence and depend heavily on circumstantial details. It also underscores the psychological toll such campaigns of intimidation can take on victims, leading to lasting fear, distrust, and disruption of daily life.

As of today, the mystery remains one of the most intriguing and unsettling cases in American criminal history, with no clear resolution in sight. The true story behind the Circleville letters, the death of Ron Gillespie, and the imprisonment of Paul Freshour may never be fully known, leaving an open chapter in the annals of unsolved crimes. The Circleville community, much like the rest of the world, continues to ponder the unanswered questions and the motives of an anonymous tormentor who, for decades, has remained an elusive figure in the shadows of this bizarre and troubling case.

Chapter 39: The Death of Princess Diana Conspiracy

The tragic death of Princess Diana, Princess of Wales, in a car crash in Paris on August 31, 1997, has been a subject of intense public scrutiny and numerous conspiracy theories. The official account, following a lengthy investigation, attributed the crash to reckless driving by Henri Paul, the driver of the Mercedes-Benz W140 carrying Diana, her companion Dodi Fayed, and bodyguard Trevor Rees-Jones. The car crashed in the Pont de l'Alma tunnel while being pursued by paparazzi, resulting in the deaths of Diana, Fayed, and Paul, with Rees-Jones being the sole survivor.

Despite the official conclusion that the crash was an accident caused by Paul's intoxication and the excessive speed at which he was driving, conspiracy theories abound. Many of these theories suggest a cover-up or a deliberate attempt to harm Diana. A central figure in these theories is Mohamed Al-Fayed, Dodi's father, who has long maintained that the British royal family and British intelligence orchestrated the crash. He suggested that the establishment could not tolerate the possibility of Diana marrying a Muslim and potentially having a child with him, which would complicate royal succession.

One of the most persistent claims involves the idea that Diana was pregnant with Dodi Fayed's child at the time of her death. This theory posits that the British establishment, fearing the implications of such a union, decided to eliminate Diana. However, subsequent investigations, including those by French authorities and Operation Paget (a British Metropolitan Police inquiry into the allegations), found no evidence to support these claims. Autopsy reports also confirmed that Diana was not pregnant.

Another theory revolves around the mysterious "white Fiat Uno" that some witnesses claimed to have seen in the tunnel at the time of the crash. The vehicle reportedly brushed against the Mercedes, causing the fatal crash. The driver of the Fiat Uno was never conclusively identified, leading to speculation that this vehicle played a critical role in a deliberate act to cause the crash. However, investigations into the Fiat Uno theory, including examinations of potential suspect vehicles and drivers, did not yield definitive evidence to support these claims.

The role of Henri Paul, the driver, is also a significant aspect of the conspiracy theories. The theories question the narrative that Paul was intoxicated, suggesting instead that he might have been an intelligence operative, possibly working for British or French intelligence. Critics argue that the evidence of his intoxication could have been manipulated or fabricated. However, toxicology reports consistently indicated high levels of alcohol and traces of prescription drugs in Paul's system, which the official investigation concluded impaired his driving ability.

Furthermore, some theories propose that the paparazzi pursuing the car were part of a coordinated effort to cause the crash. These theories suggest that the paparazzi, who had been following Diana closely during her time in France, were acting under orders from higher authorities to harass her and create a dangerous situation. However, this line of inquiry has not been substantiated, and the actions of the paparazzi, while aggressive, were generally consistent with the type of behavior expected from media photographers chasing high-profile figures.

The conspiracy theories gained additional momentum from Diana's own words. In a letter written in 1995, she expressed fears that there was a plot to tamper with her car's brakes to cause an accident. This letter, later revealed by her butler Paul Burrell, fueled speculation that Diana had been deliberately targeted. While her concerns were noted, there was no concrete evidence found during the investigations to substantiate the existence of such a plot.

Another aspect of the conspiracy theories involves the response of the emergency services and the hospital treatment Diana received. Some theories suggest that there was a deliberate delay in getting medical help to her or that she received substandard care, which contributed to her death. However, medical experts and investigators concluded that the injuries Diana sustained were extremely severe and that her chances of survival were slim, irrespective of the response time or medical care provided.

Despite extensive investigations, including the French judicial inquiry and Operation Paget, which collectively amassed thousands of pages of documentation and testimony, the conspiracy theories surrounding Diana's death have not been conclusively proven or disproven. The official stance remains that Diana's death was a tragic accident caused by a combination of factors, including the paparazzi chase, Henri Paul's impaired state, and the high speed at which the car was traveling.

The persistence of these conspiracy theories can be attributed to a combination of Diana's iconic status, public distrust in official narratives, and the unusual circumstances surrounding the event. Diana was a beloved figure, often dubbed the "People's Princess," and her death left a profound impact on many. The public's fascination with her life, combined with her tumultuous relationship with the British royal family, has led many to question the circumstances of her death, despite the lack of conclusive evidence supporting foul play.

Chapter 40: The Case of the Severed Feet

The Case of the Severed Feet, often referred to as the "Salish Sea human foot discoveries," is one of the most perplexing and eerie mysteries in recent history. This phenomenon involves human feet, usually in athletic shoes, washing ashore along the coastlines of the Salish Sea in British Columbia, Canada, and the state of Washington, United States. The first discovery was made on August 20, 2007, when a girl found a size 12 Adidas sneaker containing a human foot on Jedediah Island in British Columbia. Since then, at least 21 feet have been found, with most being in a similar state: a single foot inside a shoe, severed at the ankle or just above it.

The immediate reaction to these discoveries ranged from fear and speculation to morbid curiosity. The initial public and media response included numerous theories, from the macabre to the fantastical. Some speculated that the feet were the remains of victims of a serial killer, while others proposed they belonged to individuals who had drowned at sea. The isolated and specific nature of these findings—single feet, all in similar types of shoes—fueled theories that the severings were intentional, possibly the work of an unknown criminal.

However, forensic investigations and the work of oceanographers have provided more grounded explanations. A key factor in understanding the mystery is the buoyant nature of modern sneakers. These shoes are often designed with materials like foam and rubber, which can float. When a body decomposes in water, the soft tissues and joints break down due to natural processes. The feet, protected by shoes, are more likely to remain intact while the rest of the body decomposes or is scavenged by marine life. The shoes, buoyant and water-resistant, eventually rise to the surface and drift with the currents, eventually washing ashore.

Another significant aspect of this mystery is the geography of the Salish Sea and the surrounding coastline. The region is known for its complex tidal patterns and ocean currents, which can carry debris over long distances and deposit it on shores in seemingly random locations. The Strait of Georgia, Puget Sound, and other bodies of water in this area have currents that can transport floating objects, including these shoe-encased feet, across vast areas, often leading to their discovery far from their original location.

Despite these scientific explanations, the case has continued to intrigue the public, partly because not all feet have been conclusively identified. While advances in DNA testing have allowed authorities to match some feet to missing persons, in several instances, the remains have not been identified, adding to the air of mystery. The unidentified feet raise questions about who these individuals were and how they came to meet their end.

The case has also brought attention to various missing persons reports and unsolved disappearances in the region. For instance, some of the identified feet have been linked to individuals who were known to have drowned or were presumed dead in accidents. This has provided some closure to the families of the deceased, but in other cases, the lack of identification has only deepened the mystery. There is also the grim reality that some of these feet might belong to people whose disappearances were never reported, or to individuals who might have led isolated lives, leaving few clues about their identities.

The phenomenon has been the subject of various studies and theories, some of which are more speculative than others. For example, some researchers have suggested that a tsunami or other large-scale oceanographic event might have dislodged the bodies from underwater graves, setting them adrift. Others have pointed to the possibility of foul play, though there is no substantial evidence to support this theory beyond the coincidental fact that these discoveries all involve feet and shoes.

Media coverage and public fascination with the case have also led to a fair amount of misinformation and sensationalism. Early reports sometimes failed to note the logical explanations provided by experts, focusing instead on the more lurid aspects of the story. This has contributed to the case's status as a modern urban legend, with rumors and theories continuing to circulate despite efforts to provide scientific clarity.

Additionally, the case has had some unfortunate consequences, including hoaxes. There have been instances where people have placed animal bones inside shoes and left them on beaches, leading to false alarms and wasting police resources. These actions underscore the macabre curiosity that the case has inspired, as well as the sometimes unfortunate human tendency to exploit such situations for attention.

Chapter 41: The Smiley Face Killers Theory

The Smiley Face Killers theory is a controversial and widely debated hypothesis that suggests a group of serial killers, operating in the United States, is responsible for the deaths of numerous young men. These deaths, often classified as accidental drownings, have occurred across several states, predominantly in the Midwest and Northeast, since the late 1990s. The theory derives its name from the recurring discovery of smiley face graffiti near the locations where the bodies were found, which some believe is a signature left by the supposed killers.

The theory first gained public attention through the work of two retired New York City detectives, Kevin Gannon and Anthony Duarte, along with Dr. Lee Gilbertson, a criminal justice professor. They began investigating these cases after the 1997 disappearance and death of Patrick McNeill, a college student from Fordham University. McNeill's body was discovered in the East River, and while his death was ruled an accidental drowning, Gannon and Duarte believed there were inconsistencies and signs of foul play. Their investigation led them to connect McNeill's case with other similar incidents, sparking the idea of a nationwide conspiracy.

According to the proponents of the Smiley Face Killers theory, these deaths share several key characteristics. The victims are typically college-aged white males, athletic, academically successful, and with no history of mental illness or suicidal tendencies. They are often last seen leaving bars or parties, seemingly intoxicated, before disappearing. Their bodies are usually found in bodies of water weeks or months later, often at a distance from where they were last seen. The conditions of the bodies and the circumstances of their discovery sometimes suggest they were held or moved post-mortem, challenging the official determinations of accidental drowning.

The presence of smiley face graffiti near the discovery sites of the bodies is one of the most provocative elements of the theory. Gannon, Duarte, and Gilbertson argue that these markings are a deliberate signature left by the killers, akin to the calling cards left by some serial killers to taunt authorities. They posit that the graffiti, which varies in style and presentation, indicates an organized group of perpetrators communicating through a coded system.

The theory suggests a complex and chilling modus operandi. It proposes that the killers target young men who fit a specific profile, abduct them, and then stage their deaths to look like accidental drownings. The smiley face symbols are believed to be left as a taunting message to law enforcement and the public, signifying the killers' disdain for the authorities' inability to solve these cases. The theory also posits that the killers use the victims' intoxicated state to facilitate abductions, taking advantage of vulnerable moments when the young men are separated from friends and less capable of defending themselves.

However, the Smiley Face Killers theory has been met with significant skepticism and criticism from both law enforcement and independent experts. Critics argue that the theory lacks concrete evidence and is primarily based on circumstantial connections and speculation. They point out that smiley face graffiti is a common and easily recognizable symbol, making it an unreliable indicator of a linked series of crimes. Additionally, the theory has been criticized for not providing sufficient forensic or physical evidence to support the claims of abduction and foul play.

Many of the cases cited by proponents of the theory have been independently reviewed and reaffirmed as accidental drownings. Investigations often reveal that the young men had consumed significant amounts of alcohol, impairing their judgment and coordination, which could lead to accidental falls into water. Furthermore, autopsies and toxicology reports in several cases have not supported the presence of drugs or other substances that might suggest incapacitation or foul play.

The FBI and other law enforcement agencies have publicly stated that they do not support the Smiley Face Killers theory, noting that there is no credible evidence of a nationwide conspiracy or a network of serial killers responsible for these deaths. They argue that while each case is tragic and deserves thorough investigation, the similarities in victim profiles and circumstances can be explained by common social behaviors, such as young men drinking at bars and walking near bodies of water.

Despite these official positions, the Smiley Face Killers theory has continued to capture public interest. This enduring fascination can be attributed to the unsettling nature of the cases and the human tendency to seek patterns and explanations for mysterious or unexplained events. The idea of an organized group of killers preying on seemingly random victims taps into deep-seated fears about safety and vulnerability, especially in urban environments where young people often socialize.

The theory has also been fueled by media coverage, including documentaries, news specials, and true crime programs that highlight the cases and the debate surrounding the theory. These portrayals often emphasize the unexplained aspects of the deaths and the eerie coincidences, which can overshadow the more mundane explanations provided by official investigations. The tension between the sensational elements of the theory and the prosaic realities of the cases continues to make the Smiley Face Killers a topic of public intrigue and speculation.

Chapter 42: The Disappearance of Lars Mittank

The disappearance of Lars Mittank is one of the most baffling and widely publicized missing person cases in recent years, often described as the "most famous missing person on YouTube." Lars Mittank, a 28-year-old German man, vanished on July 8, 2014, under mysterious circumstances from the Varna Airport in Bulgaria. His disappearance has sparked numerous theories and intense online speculation, partly due to the eerie and inexplicable nature of the events leading up to it, which were captured on surveillance cameras.

Lars Mittank traveled to the Bulgarian resort of Golden Sands with a group of friends for a vacation. The trip seemed to be going well until Lars got involved in a physical altercation on July 6, 2014, outside a local bar. The exact details of the fight remain unclear, but it allegedly involved a dispute over football, with Lars supporting the German team while the locals supported another. During the scuffle, Lars suffered an injury to his ear, which later resulted in a ruptured eardrum. Due to this injury, a doctor advised him not to fly, as changes in air pressure could aggravate his condition.

Lars decided to stay behind in Bulgaria while his friends returned to Germany, planning to travel back by another means once he was cleared to fly. He checked into the Hotel Color in Varna, where his behavior began to take a strange turn. According to hotel staff and his communications with his mother, Sandra Mittank, Lars appeared increasingly paranoid and agitated. He claimed that four men were following him and that he feared for his life. He sent text messages to his mother expressing concern and asked her to cancel his credit cards, suggesting that he was in danger. However, there was no evidence to support his claims, and the hotel staff did not notice any suspicious individuals.

On July 8, Lars visited a doctor at the Varna Airport Medical Center to get clearance to fly. The doctor noted that Lars appeared nervous and agitated, and during the consultation, he abruptly left the office, leaving behind his luggage, passport, and other personal belongings. Surveillance footage from the airport captured Lars exiting the building in a state of apparent distress. He was seen walking through the airport, running across the terminal, and eventually scaling a fence to leave the airport grounds, heading into a nearby field and disappearing into a wooded area. This footage became the last confirmed sighting of Lars Mittank, and despite extensive searches, he has not been seen since.

The disappearance of Lars Mittank has led to numerous theories and speculations. One of the most prominent theories suggests that Lars was experiencing a psychological episode, possibly exacerbated by the head injury he sustained during the altercation or by an underlying mental health condition. Some have speculated that he may have been experiencing a form of paranoia or psychosis, which could explain his erratic behavior, fear of being followed, and sudden flight from the airport.

Another theory posits that Lars was under the influence of a drug that caused paranoia or hallucinations. There is speculation that he may have inadvertently ingested a substance, either through medication or food, that affected his mental state. This theory is bolstered by the fact that Lars had been prescribed antibiotics for his ear injury, and it is conceivable that he could have had an adverse reaction to the medication, though this remains speculative.

There is also the possibility that Lars was indeed in danger, as he claimed. Some theorists suggest that he might have encountered individuals involved in criminal activities, possibly related to drug trafficking or human trafficking, which led to his fear and eventual disappearance. However, there has been no corroborating evidence to support this theory, and local authorities have found no indications of such a threat during their investigations.

The case has been further complicated by various reported sightings of Lars across Europe, though none have been substantiated. These reports, along with the extensive media coverage and online interest in the case, have led to numerous leads, but none have resulted in a confirmed sighting or location of Lars. His family, particularly his mother, has remained actively involved in the search, appealing for information and maintaining hope that he might still be found.

In addition to these theories, there is the grim possibility that Lars met with foul play or suffered an accident after leaving the airport. The area he disappeared into includes both rural and urban landscapes, with potential hazards such as traffic, waterways, and rough terrain. It's possible that he succumbed to exposure, injury, or another misadventure, although extensive searches have not uncovered any remains or belongings.

The disappearance of Lars Mittank continues to intrigue and baffle people worldwide, partly due to the lack of clear answers and the unsettling nature of the airport surveillance footage. The case has been widely discussed in true crime forums, documentaries, and YouTube channels, where amateur sleuths and armchair detectives pore over the available evidence and speculate on Lars's fate. Despite the public interest and numerous theories, the case remains unsolved, with Lars Mittank officially listed as a missing person.

Chapter 43: The Boy in the Box

The Boy in the Box, also known as "America's Unknown Child," is one of the most enduring and perplexing cold cases in American history. This case involves the discovery of the body of an unidentified boy, estimated to be between four and six years old, in a cardboard box in Philadelphia, Pennsylvania. The boy's body was found on February 25, 1957, and despite extensive efforts by law enforcement, the media, and the public, his identity and the circumstances surrounding his death remain unknown.

The case began when a young man checking his muskrat traps in a rural area known as Fox Chase, Philadelphia, came across a cardboard box partially covered with a blanket. Inside the box was the nude, battered body of a young boy. The box itself was identified as having once contained a bassinet sold by J.C. Penney, but no further identifying information was found. The boy's body bore signs of prolonged abuse, including bruises, scars, and indications of malnutrition. His hair had been crudely cut close to the scalp, possibly after his death, as clumps of hair were found on the body and in the box.

The discovery of the boy's body triggered an intensive investigation. The Philadelphia Police Department, with assistance from local and national agencies, pursued numerous leads, canvassed the area, and distributed over 400,000 flyers featuring a sketch of the boy and the box in hopes of identifying him. The flyers were posted in police stations, post offices, and public places, and even included in utility bills. Despite these efforts, no one came forward with credible information about the boy's identity or how he ended up in the box.

The autopsy conducted by Dr. Joseph W. Spelman revealed that the boy had died from blunt force trauma to the head. There were also signs of multiple older injuries and scars, suggesting a history of physical abuse. Some scars indicated surgical procedures, possibly on the chest and groin. However, there were no conclusive findings to identify a specific cause for the injuries. The boy's esophagus contained a dark, brown residue, which led to speculation that he might have vomited shortly before his death, possibly as a result of a recent meal. His stomach contents, however, were inconclusive.

The police explored various avenues in their investigation, including tracking down the origins of the cardboard box and the blanket found with the body. The box had been shipped to a J.C. Penney store in Upper Darby, Pennsylvania, but no records were found of who purchased the bassinet it had contained. The blanket, made of cheap cotton flannel and printed with a distinctive diamond pattern, was also traced to a manufacturer in North Carolina, but the trail went cold as the blanket was a common, mass-produced item. Additionally, the boy's fingerprints and footprints were taken, but there were no matches in any databases, and dental records also provided no clues.

Over the years, several theories and potential leads have emerged, though none have conclusively solved the mystery. One theory suggested that the boy might have been a foster child or had been abandoned by his parents, potentially explaining the lack of identification. Another theory proposed that he was a victim of a human trafficking ring, though this idea also lacked concrete evidence. There were also speculations about the boy being an immigrant or coming from a transient family, which might explain why no one came forward to claim him.

In the early stages of the investigation, a psychic led police to a foster home not far from where the boy was found. The psychic described a house that matched the foster home, and the owners had purchased a similar bassinet, which raised suspicions. However, after a thorough investigation, including questioning the foster parents and checking the welfare of the children in their care, the police found no evidence connecting them to the boy.

Another significant development came in 2002 when a woman identified only as "M" came forward, claiming that her abusive mother had bought the boy, named "Jonathan," from his birth parents in 1954. According to M, the boy was subjected to extreme physical and sexual abuse for two and a half years before being killed in a fit of rage. M's account included details that seemed consistent with the known facts of the case, including the boy's appearance and the circumstances of his discovery. However, there was skepticism about her story, as M had a history of mental illness, and police could not corroborate the details of her account with any physical evidence.

Despite these leads, the case has never been conclusively solved. Advances in forensic science, particularly in DNA analysis, have provided new avenues for investigation. In 1998, the boy's body was exhumed to obtain DNA samples, which were added to national databases in hopes of finding a match. As of the latest updates, there has been no conclusive match, though the DNA could still potentially lead to identification as more people submit their genetic information to databases for genealogical purposes.

The case has also inspired widespread public interest and numerous theories proposed by amateur sleuths and crime enthusiasts. Some have speculated that the boy might have been a member of a traveling circus or a migrant worker's family, potentially explaining why no one reported him missing. Others have suggested that he could have been raised in an institutional setting, such as an orphanage, where his mistreatment might have gone unnoticed.

The Boy in the Box remains a haunting and unresolved mystery, symbolizing the countless unsolved cases of missing and unidentified persons. Despite the passage of time, the case continues to attract attention, with investigators, journalists, and the public holding out hope that one day, the boy's identity and the circumstances of his death will be uncovered. The case is a poignant reminder of the importance of child protection and the often invisible suffering of vulnerable children. The continued efforts to solve the case, including renewed investigations and the application of modern forensic techniques, reflect a commitment to seeking justice for the young boy who has come to be known only as "America's Unknown Child."

Chapter 44: The Unsolved Lindow Man

The Unsolved Lindow Man, also known as "Pete Marsh," is one of the most remarkable and enigmatic archaeological finds in British history. Discovered in a peat bog near Lindow Moss in Cheshire, England, in 1984, the well-preserved body of this ancient man has provided a fascinating glimpse into the past. Despite extensive studies and analyses, many aspects of Lindow Man's life and death remain shrouded in mystery, making it an enduring topic of intrigue for archaeologists, historians, and the public.

The discovery of Lindow Man was accidental, occurring during commercial peat extraction. On August 1, 1984, workers at the site unearthed a preserved human foot, initially believed to be a modern homicide victim. The police were called, and further excavation revealed the rest of the body, which was later identified as that of an adult male, estimated to have lived around 2,000 years ago during the Iron Age or Romano-British period. The peat bog had created an anaerobic environment, remarkably preserving the body, which became known as a "bog body."

Lindow Man's preservation was extraordinary, allowing researchers to study various aspects of his physical characteristics, health, and potential causes of death. He was approximately 25 years old at the time of his death, stood about 5 feet 6 inches tall, and had a slight build. His hair and beard were well-groomed, and his fingernails were manicured, suggesting that he was of a higher social status and did not engage in manual labor. These details offer a rare insight into the appearance and personal grooming habits of people from his time.

One of the most intriguing aspects of Lindow Man is the evidence of a violent death. The body showed multiple signs of trauma, leading to various theories about the cause of death and the circumstances surrounding it. He had a depressed fracture at the top of his skull, suggesting a blow to the head, likely inflicted by a blunt instrument.

Additionally, there were ligature marks around his neck, indicating strangulation, and a cut to the throat. The presence of these injuries has led some researchers to propose that Lindow Man may have been a victim of ritual sacrifice, a practice not uncommon in Iron Age Europe.

The theory of ritual sacrifice is supported by the presence of mistletoe pollen in Lindow Man's stomach, an important plant in Druidic religious practices. This finding suggests that he may have consumed a ritual drink containing mistletoe before his death. Some researchers believe that Lindow Man's death may have been a "threefold death," a form of ritual killing described in ancient texts where the victim dies by three different means—bludgeoning, strangulation, and throat-cutting—all of which are present in Lindow Man's case. This ritualistic interpretation aligns with known practices among Celtic societies, where sacrifices were sometimes made to appease gods or during significant religious or political events.

However, the interpretation of Lindow Man's death as a ritual sacrifice is not without controversy. Some scholars argue that the evidence does not conclusively point to ritualistic motives and that the injuries could result from interpersonal violence, execution, or even a form of punishment. The lack of conclusive evidence about the social or cultural context of Lindow Man's death leaves room for multiple interpretations. The debate over the nature of his death highlights the challenges of reconstructing historical events from limited archaeological evidence.

In addition to the violent injuries, Lindow Man's body showed signs of other physical ailments and conditions. He suffered from intestinal parasites, including whipworm and maw worm, which were common in ancient populations due to poor hygiene and diet. Analysis of his fingernails and hair revealed a relatively high-protein diet, including meat, which was not typical for the general population during his time. This dietary detail, along with his well-groomed appearance, suggests that Lindow Man may have been a person of some importance or had access to resources that were not widely available.

Lindow Man's discovery has provided invaluable insights into the life and death of people in Iron Age Britain. However, it has also raised many questions about the social, cultural, and religious practices of the time. The lack of written records from this period means that much of what we understand is based on archaeological evidence, which can be open to interpretation. The study of Lindow Man continues to evolve as new technologies and methodologies become available, offering the potential for further revelations about his life and the society he lived in.

The public and academic interest in Lindow Man has led to several exhibitions and publications, bringing together a wide range of disciplines, including archaeology, anthropology, forensic science, and history. These collaborative efforts aim to build a more comprehensive picture of Lindow Man's world, shedding light on the broader context of his existence and the cultural practices of Iron Age Britain.

Despite the extensive study, Lindow Man remains an unsolved enigma. His well-preserved body has provided a wealth of information, yet key aspects of his life and death continue to elude definitive explanation. The mystery of his identity, the precise circumstances of his death, and the reasons behind his apparent violent end remain open to speculation and interpretation. The ongoing fascination with Lindow Man reflects a broader human interest in the past and the stories that ancient remains can tell us about our ancestors.

Chapter 45: The Great Train Robbery

The Great Train Robbery is one of the most infamous and audacious crimes in British history, capturing the public's imagination with its blend of meticulous planning, high-stakes execution, and colorful cast of characters. The robbery took place on the night of August 8, 1963, when a gang of 15 men, led by Bruce Reynolds, targeted a Royal Mail train traveling from Glasgow to London. The gang successfully intercepted the train, making off with a haul of £2.6 million, equivalent to over £50 million today. The heist became legendary not only for the scale of the theft but also for the dramatic escape and the subsequent capture of many of the perpetrators.

The planning of the Great Train Robbery began months in advance, with Bruce Reynolds, a seasoned criminal known for his meticulous attention to detail, orchestrating the operation. The gang gathered information on the train's schedule, security arrangements, and the layout of the carriages. They learned that large amounts of cash were regularly transported on the train, primarily consisting of money being returned to London banks after the Scottish Bank Holiday. This cash was carried in High Value Packages (HVPs), which were stored in a secure carriage towards the front of the train.

Reynolds assembled a team of skilled criminals, each bringing specific expertise to the operation. This included Gordon Goody, a professional thief; Charlie Wilson, known for his criminal connections; Roy James, a racing driver and expert in getaway tactics; and Ronald "Buster" Edwards, a petty criminal and former boxer. The gang also enlisted the help of a retired train driver, known only as "Stan Agate," or "the Ulsterman," to assist in moving the train during the robbery.

The plan involved stopping the train at a remote location, called Bridego Bridge, near Ledburn in Buckinghamshire. To achieve this, the gang tampered with the signals to turn a green signal to red, causing the train to halt. The plan required precise timing and coordination, as the gang had to control the train and its crew quickly to avoid detection. To accomplish this, they incapacitated the train driver, Jack Mills, by hitting him over the head with a cosh, rendering him semi-conscious. While this action drew significant public sympathy for Mills, it also highlighted the gang's willingness to use violence to achieve their goal.

With the train stopped and the crew subdued, the gang uncoupled the HVP carriage and transported it about half a mile to Bridego Bridge using "Stan Agate's" driving skills. There, they formed a human chain to unload the bags of cash, which they then transported to waiting vehicles. The entire operation took just 30 minutes, showcasing the gang's efficiency and preparation. They left behind the injured Jack Mills and his co-driver David Whitby, both of whom were later found and provided descriptions of the gang.

After the robbery, the gang retreated to Leatherslade Farm, a remote farmhouse they had rented as a hideout. They had planned to lay low there for several weeks while the heat died down. However, the sheer scale of the robbery quickly made headlines, and the police launched an extensive investigation. Despite their efforts to clean up and leave no trace, the gang's presence at the farmhouse was discovered due to a combination of forensic evidence and tips from the public. This evidence included fingerprints on a Monopoly board the gang had played with during their stay and the gang's careless disposal of the HVP bags and other items.

The investigation, led by Detective Chief Superintendent Tommy Butler and his Flying Squad team, resulted in the eventual capture and conviction of most of the gang members. Bruce Reynolds managed to evade capture for several years, living a life on the run across various countries before finally being arrested in 1968. Other members, like Ronnie Biggs, became famous for their dramatic escapes and subsequent life on the run. Biggs's escape from Wandsworth Prison in

1965 and his eventual flight to Brazil became legendary, adding to the mystique and folklore surrounding the robbery.

The trial of the Great Train Robbers was one of the longest and most publicized in British legal history. It began in January 1964 at Aylesbury Assizes and featured tight security, including the presence of armed guards and police dogs. The proceedings attracted massive media attention, with the defendants becoming minor celebrities. The trial concluded in March 1964, with eleven men being convicted and sentenced to lengthy prison terms. The severity of the sentences, ranging from 20 to 30 years, was intended to send a strong message against such brazen criminal activities.

Despite the successful capture and prosecution of many of the robbers, the case left a lasting impact on British society and culture. The public was both horrified and fascinated by the robbery, leading to numerous books, films, and documentaries. The robbery highlighted issues within the British transport and postal security systems, leading to reforms to prevent similar incidents in the future. It also raised questions about the romanticization of criminals, as many of the robbers were portrayed as folk heroes, particularly Ronnie Biggs, whose life on the run became a media sensation.

The Great Train Robbery's cultural impact extended beyond the immediate aftermath. It inspired various works of fiction and became a reference point in discussions of crime and justice. The robbery's details, such as the use of the red signal and the coshing of Jack Mills, entered popular consciousness. The gang members' personas, especially their criminal sophistication and audacity, influenced public perceptions of crime and criminals, sometimes glamorizing the darker aspects of their actions.

In the decades following the robbery, many of the key figures involved died or served their sentences and faded from the public eye. Bruce Reynolds, often considered the mastermind behind the operation, was released from prison in 1978 and later wrote memoirs detailing his life and the robbery. He passed away in 2013. Ronnie Biggs lived as a fugitive in Brazil for many years before voluntarily returning to the UK in 2001, where he was re-imprisoned until his release on compassionate grounds in 2009. He died in 2013, shortly after Reynolds, marking the end of an era for the remaining members of the gang.

The Great Train Robbery remains a defining moment in British criminal history, symbolizing a period of audacious, high-stakes crime that seemed to capture the imagination of the public. It stands as a testament to the complexities of crime, justice, and media representation. While the gang's actions caused significant harm, including to the train driver Jack Mills, who suffered lifelong health issues due to the attack, the narrative surrounding the robbery has often focused on the ingenuity and boldness of the perpetrators. This duality reflects broader societal attitudes toward crime and punishment, as well as the allure of the "gentleman criminal" archetype.

Chapter 46: The Disappearance of Emanuela Orlandi

The disappearance of Emanuela Orlandi is one of Italy's most enduring and perplexing mysteries, involving the Vatican, organized crime, international intrigue, and a swirl of conspiracy theories. Emanuela Orlandi was a 15-year-old Vatican citizen who vanished on June 22, 1983, under mysterious circumstances. Her case has captivated Italy and the world for decades, not only because of its tragic nature but also because of the complex web of potential motives, suspects, and theories that have emerged over the years.

Emanuela Orlandi was the daughter of Ercole Orlandi, a Vatican employee who worked as a clerk in the Prefecture of the Papal Household. The family lived within the Vatican City, which is an independent city-state surrounded by Rome. On the day of her disappearance, Emanuela left her home to attend a music lesson in Rome, as she was an aspiring flautist. She usually took the bus to her music school, the Tommaso Ludovico Da Victoria School, located near the Vatican. According to reports, Emanuela called her sister from a public phone booth to say she had been approached by a man offering her a job promoting Avon cosmetics. This was the last time her family heard from her.

When Emanuela failed to return home, her family became concerned and reported her missing. The initial response from the authorities was somewhat lackluster, as it was common at the time to assume that a teenage girl might have run away or was simply delayed. However, as days turned into weeks, and then months, the lack of any communication or ransom demands made it clear that something more sinister had occurred. The Vatican, the Italian police, and the media became involved in the search, but no concrete evidence of her whereabouts or fate emerged.

The disappearance quickly became a major news story, and various theories began to circulate. One of the earliest theories suggested that Emanuela had been kidnapped by a criminal organization in an attempt to pressure the Vatican. At the time, the Vatican Bank was embroiled in a major financial scandal involving the collapse of Banco Ambrosiano, an Italian bank with close ties to the Vatican. Roberto Calvi, known as "God's Banker," was found dead in London under mysterious circumstances, and there were allegations of Mafia involvement. Some speculated that Emanuela's abduction was related to this financial scandal, possibly as leverage against the Vatican to recover lost funds or to silence certain individuals.

Another major theory proposed that Emanuela was kidnapped as a bargaining chip to secure the release of Mehmet Ali Ağca, the Turkish man who attempted to assassinate Pope John Paul II in 1981. Ağca was a member of the Grey Wolves, a far-right Turkish nationalist group, and there was speculation that the kidnapping could have been orchestrated to secure his release from prison. This theory gained traction when a man claiming to represent the "Turkish Anti-Christian Liberation Front" called an Italian news agency and demanded Ağca's release in exchange for information on Emanuela's whereabouts. However, no concrete evidence emerged to support this connection, and the identity and motives of the caller were never confirmed.

The case took another twist when in 1985, two years after Emanuela's disappearance, a young girl named Mirella Gregori also went missing in Rome under similar circumstances. This led to speculation that the two cases might be connected, although no definitive link was ever established. The similarities between the two disappearances further fueled rumors of a broader conspiracy or the involvement of a serial kidnapper.

Over the years, numerous people have come forward claiming to have information about Emanuela's fate, including some who alleged that she was still alive. In the 1990s, an anonymous caller to the Italian television program "Chi l'ha visto?" claimed that Emanuela had been abducted and was being held by a Vatican-linked organization. The caller also suggested that the answer to the mystery lay in the tomb of Enrico De Pedis, a notorious Roman gangster who was buried in the Basilica of Sant'Apollinare, a location not far from where Emanuela was last seen. This led to widespread speculation that the Mafia might have been involved in her disappearance.

In 2012, Italian authorities, acting on a tip from an anonymous source, exhumed De Pedis's tomb in the hopes of finding clues about Emanuela's disappearance. While nothing directly related to Emanuela was found, the fact that a criminal like De Pedis was buried in a basilica raised further questions about the possible links between organized crime, the Vatican, and the disappearance. The Vatican's involvement in the case, or lack thereof, has been a subject of intense scrutiny and criticism over the years. The Orlandi family, particularly Emanuela's brother Pietro, has been vocal in accusing the Vatican of not fully cooperating with the investigation or releasing all the information it might have. The family's quest for answers has included multiple public appeals, meetings with Vatican officials, and even direct appeals to various Popes, including Pope Francis.

In recent years, the case has seen renewed interest, partly due to the release of books, documentaries, and films exploring various aspects of the mystery. In 2019, the Vatican allowed two ossuaries in the Teutonic Cemetery within Vatican City to be opened after the Orlandi family received an anonymous tip suggesting that Emanuela's remains might be there. The search did not yield any conclusive evidence, but it underscored the enduring nature of the mystery and the family's relentless pursuit of answers.

The disappearance of Emanuela Orlandi has become a symbol of broader issues related to the Vatican's transparency and accountability. The case has prompted discussions about the Vatican's handling of internal affairs, including financial scandals, allegations of corruption, and the church's response to criminal activities. It has also highlighted the complexities of Vatican-Italian relations, as the case straddles issues of jurisdiction and diplomatic sensitivity.

As of today, the fate of Emanuela Orlandi remains unknown, and her disappearance continues to be one of the most puzzling and enduring mysteries of modern times. The case has spawned numerous conspiracy theories, some of which suggest involvement by high-ranking Vatican officials, secret societies, or even foreign intelligence agencies. Despite the passage of time, the case remains a potent symbol of unresolved justice and the often opaque nature of Vatican affairs.

Chapter 47: The Unsolved Gardner Museum Heist

The Isabella Stewart Gardner Museum Heist, often described as one of the most notorious art thefts in history, occurred in the early hours of March 18, 1990, in Boston, Massachusetts. The heist involved the theft of 13 pieces of art, valued at around $500 million, making it the largest property theft in the world at the time. Despite numerous investigations, tips, and even a $10 million reward, the stolen artworks have never been recovered, and the case remains unsolved to this day.

The Isabella Stewart Gardner Museum is a renowned art museum established by its namesake, Isabella Stewart Gardner, a prominent art collector and philanthropist, in 1903. The museum is housed in a building designed to resemble a Venetian palazzo and contains a diverse collection of art, including paintings, sculptures, tapestries, and decorative arts. The collection includes works by masters such as Rembrandt, Vermeer, Degas, Manet, and others, making it a significant cultural and artistic treasure.

The heist took place on the night following St. Patrick's Day, a time when the city of Boston is known for its festivities and celebrations. At around 1:24 AM, two men dressed as Boston police officers arrived at the museum's side entrance. The museum had minimal security measures in place at the time, with only two unarmed guards on duty. The thieves convinced the guards that they were responding to a disturbance call, a ruse that played into the guards' sense of duty and routine. Once inside, the impostors quickly overpowered the guards, handcuffing and binding them in the museum's basement.

With the guards neutralized, the thieves had free rein to execute their meticulously planned theft. The heist lasted approximately 81 minutes, during which the thieves methodically selected and removed specific pieces of art. The stolen items included Vermeer's "The

Concert," Rembrandt's "The Storm on the Sea of Galilee" (his only known seascape), and "A Lady and Gentleman in Black," as well as works by Edgar Degas, Édouard Manet, and Johannes Vermeer. They also took a Chinese bronze gu, a finial from a Napoleonic flag, and a French imperial eagle finial. Notably, they left behind several valuable works, suggesting that they either had specific instructions or were familiar with the museum's layout and collection.

One of the most puzzling aspects of the heist is the method the thieves used to remove the paintings. Rather than carefully detaching the paintings from their frames, they cut the canvases from the frames, leaving the frames behind. This rough handling of the artwork led to speculation that the thieves were not seasoned art criminals, as such actions would significantly damage the value and integrity of the works. Additionally, the choice of artworks stolen has perplexed experts, as some more valuable pieces were left untouched.

In the aftermath of the heist, the museum and law enforcement launched an extensive investigation. The FBI took the lead in the investigation, classifying the case as a major art theft and placing it under the jurisdiction of its Art Crime Team. Despite their efforts, the investigation faced numerous challenges. The thieves left behind very few clues, and the museum's lack of security measures, such as an adequate alarm system and CCTV cameras, hindered the investigation. The museum's security tapes showed the thieves moving through the galleries, but their disguises and the limited quality of the footage provided little useful information.

Over the years, the case has seen numerous leads and theories, but none have led to the recovery of the stolen art. In the years following the heist, the FBI pursued various lines of inquiry, including potential involvement by organized crime groups, known art thieves, and even insider involvement. Some theories suggested that the art was stolen to be used as collateral for other criminal activities or to be sold in the black market. Others speculated that the theft was commissioned by a wealthy collector with a private interest in the works.

One of the most persistent theories involved the possibility of organized crime involvement, specifically the Boston Mafia. This theory gained traction due to the city's history of organized crime and the timing of the heist. The FBI investigated known figures in the Boston underworld, including James "Whitey" Bulger, a notorious crime boss, and his associates. However, despite extensive efforts, no direct links between these individuals and the heist were established. The lack of concrete evidence and the passage of time have made it increasingly difficult to track down potential suspects or recover the stolen works.

In 2013, the FBI announced that it had identified the two men responsible for the heist, suggesting they were members of a criminal organization based in New England and the Mid-Atlantic states. However, the FBI did not publicly name the suspects, citing ongoing investigations. This announcement raised hopes that the case might be nearing a resolution, but as of now, no arrests have been made, and the whereabouts of the stolen art remain unknown.

The Gardner Museum has been proactive in its efforts to recover the stolen artworks. The museum has offered a $10 million reward for information leading to the recovery of the stolen items, one of the largest private rewards ever offered. The museum has also maintained the empty frames of the stolen paintings on display, a poignant reminder of the loss and an appeal for the return of the missing works. The frames serve as both a symbol of hope and a testament to the cultural loss experienced due to the theft.

The Gardner Museum Heist has captured the public's imagination and become a focal point for discussions on art crime, security, and the black market for stolen art. The case has inspired numerous books, documentaries, and even fictional portrayals, each exploring different aspects of the heist and the world of art theft. The theft has also had a significant impact on museum security practices, prompting institutions worldwide to reevaluate their security measures and protocols to prevent similar incidents.

Despite the challenges and the passage of more than three decades, the case remains open, and both the FBI and the Gardner Museum continue to hope for a breakthrough. The museum has emphasized its commitment to pursuing any credible leads and working with law enforcement to recover the stolen pieces. The case's enduring mystery, combined with the cultural and historical significance of the stolen works, ensures that it remains a topic of fascination and investigation.

Chapter 48: The Murder of Amber Hagerman

Amber Rene Hagerman, born on November 25, 1986, was a nine-year-old girl living in Arlington, Texas. Her life was tragically cut short on January 13, 1996, in a case that remains unsolved but has had a lasting impact on child safety measures in the United States.

On that fateful day, Amber and her younger brother Ricky went for a bike ride near their grandmother's house. They rode to the abandoned Winn-Dixie grocery store parking lot, a place they often visited. Ricky decided to head back home, but Amber wanted to stay a bit longer. As she rode her bike, an unknown assailant grabbed her, threw her into a black pickup truck, and sped away. This horrifying scene was witnessed by a nearby resident, Jim Kevil, who immediately called 911. His detailed description of the abduction provided crucial information: a dark-colored pickup truck, possibly a black 1980s or early 1990s model, and a white or Hispanic male in his 20s to 30s.

The Arlington Police Department quickly responded, launching an extensive search operation involving local, state, and federal authorities. Volunteers, friends, and family members distributed flyers and conducted door-to-door searches, hoping to find any clue that could lead to Amber's safe return. The community was on high alert, with Amber's abduction dominating the local news.

Despite these efforts, four days later, on January 17, 1996, a man walking his dog discovered Amber's lifeless body in a drainage ditch near Arlington's Forest Hill Apartments, approximately four miles from where she was abducted. An autopsy revealed that Amber had been alive for at least two days after her abduction and had suffered severe injuries, including cuts and bruises. Her throat had been slit. This revelation intensified the urgency to find her killer.

Investigators combed through the evidence, hoping to find leads that would point to the perpetrator. They interviewed more than 8,000 individuals, meticulously following up on tips and potential sightings of the suspect vehicle. Despite these exhaustive efforts, the investigation yielded no significant breakthroughs. Amber's killer remained elusive, shrouded in mystery and evading justice.

As the years passed, the community and Amber's family continued to seek answers. The police did not give up, periodically re-examining the evidence with advances in forensic technology. In 2011, the Arlington Police Department partnered with the FBI to re-evaluate the case, hoping that new DNA analysis techniques could unearth new clues. However, even with these efforts, no new leads emerged.

Amber's tragic death, while deeply sorrowful, spurred significant changes in how child abductions are handled in the United States. Her mother, Donna Williams, channeled her grief into advocacy, working tirelessly to prevent other families from experiencing similar heartbreak. In the wake of Amber's murder, a crucial initiative was born: the AMBER Alert system.

Named in Amber's honor, the AMBER Alert (America's Missing: Broadcast Emergency Response) system was established to quickly disseminate information about abducted children to the public, increasing the chances of a swift and safe recovery. The program, initiated in Texas, spread nationwide and has since been adopted in various forms worldwide. It leverages the power of mass media and digital platforms, broadcasting alerts through television, radio, highway signs, and even mobile phones. The system has been credited with successfully recovering numerous abducted children, saving lives and preventing further tragedies.

Despite the enduring impact of the AMBER Alert system, the pain of Amber's unsolved case lingers. Her family, friends, and community continue to hold onto hope that one day, new evidence or a confession will bring her killer to justice. The case remains open, with law enforcement periodically revisiting the investigation, keeping Amber's memory alive in the pursuit of answers.

Amber Hagerman's story is a poignant reminder of the fragility of life and the importance of vigilance in protecting our children. Her legacy, through the AMBER Alert system, underscores the collective responsibility to respond swiftly and decisively to child abductions. It is a testament to the enduring power of community and the profound impact that one life can have on society.

The search for Amber's killer remains active, with her case still featured on various true crime platforms and cold case investigations. Each year, the Arlington Police Department reviews the evidence, hoping that advancements in forensic science will eventually lead to a breakthrough. The community continues to commemorate Amber's life, holding vigils and memorials to honor her memory and keep her story in the public consciousness.

Amber Hagerman's tragic fate is a sobering chapter in the annals of unsolved crimes, yet her legacy transcends the sorrow of her loss. Her case has galvanized efforts to protect vulnerable children, prompting systemic changes that have undoubtedly saved lives. The AMBER Alert system stands as a beacon of hope, a direct result of Amber's legacy, and a powerful tool in the fight against child abductions. While her killer may still be at large, the ripples of her life and death continue to inspire and mobilize communities, reinforcing the unyielding pursuit of justice and the unwavering commitment to safeguarding our children.

Chapter 49: The Case of the Pollock Twins

The case of the Pollock Twins, often cited in discussions about reincarnation, is one of the most intriguing and enigmatic stories of the 20th century. John and Florence Pollock lived in Hexham, England, with their two daughters, Joanna, born in 1946, and Jacqueline, born in 1951. The family lived a relatively quiet life until a tragic event in 1957 changed everything.

On May 5, 1957, Joanna and Jacqueline were walking to church with a friend when they were struck and killed by a car driven by a mentally disturbed woman who had intentionally driven onto the sidewalk. The deaths devastated the Pollock family. John and Florence were inconsolable, struggling to come to terms with the loss of their beloved daughters. During this time, John Pollock, who had a strong belief in reincarnation, began to hope that his daughters might return to them in some way.

A year later, Florence became pregnant again, and on October 4, 1958, she gave birth to twin girls, Gillian and Jennifer. The twins were identical, but there were some peculiarities that caught the attention of their parents and later investigators. Jennifer had a birthmark on her waist that closely resembled a birthmark Jacqueline had, and she also had a mark on her forehead similar to a scar Jacqueline had in the same spot. These birthmarks sparked the initial curiosity and belief in the possibility of reincarnation.

As the twins grew, more startling similarities between them and their deceased sisters emerged. Gillian and Jennifer began to exhibit behaviors and preferences that were eerily reminiscent of Joanna and Jacqueline. They asked for toys that had belonged to their older sisters, toys they had no way of knowing about. They also showed an uncanny knowledge of the Hexham streets and landmarks that they had never visited but which Joanna and Jacqueline had known well.

One of the most compelling aspects of the Pollock Twins case is the distinct memories they seemed to have of their previous lives. When the family moved back to Hexham when the twins were around four years old, they began to recognize places and landmarks that Joanna and Jacqueline had known. For instance, they correctly identified their school and the playground despite having never been there before. Additionally, they would point out locations where Joanna and Jacqueline had visited frequently, further convincing their parents of the possibility of reincarnation.

The twins also exhibited unusual phobias and behaviors that aligned with the events leading up to Joanna and Jacqueline's deaths. They had a strong fear of cars, which seemed to stem from the traumatic accident that had killed their sisters. Whenever a car engine started, they would become anxious and cling to their parents, a behavior that was unusual for children who had not experienced such a traumatic event firsthand.

John Pollock's belief in reincarnation was reinforced by these experiences, and he began to share the story with researchers and the public. The case attracted the attention of Dr. Ian Stevenson, a psychiatrist from the University of Virginia who was known for his work in studying reincarnation. Dr. Stevenson conducted extensive interviews with the Pollock family and documented the case in detail, considering it one of the most convincing cases of reincarnation he had encountered.

Dr. Stevenson noted that the Pollock Twins exhibited not only physical similarities to their deceased sisters but also behavioral and psychological traits that seemed to transcend their current lives. His research included detailed comparisons of the twins' behaviors, preferences, and memories with those of Joanna and Jacqueline. Dr.

Stevenson found that the twins' recollections were too specific and accurate to be dismissed as mere coincidences or parental influence.

Critics of the reincarnation theory have argued that the similarities could be attributed to parental influence or environmental factors. They suggest that John and Florence Pollock, consciously or unconsciously, might have projected memories and behaviors onto the twins, thus shaping their development. However, Dr. Stevenson and other researchers have countered these claims by pointing out the specific and accurate nature of the twins' memories, which could not easily be explained by environmental factors alone.

As the Pollock Twins grew older, their memories of their past lives began to fade, a phenomenon commonly observed in cases of alleged reincarnation. By the age of seven, most of their memories of being Joanna and Jacqueline had dissipated, and they began to develop their own distinct personalities and lives. Despite this, the early years of Gillian and Jennifer's lives remain a subject of fascination and debate among researchers and skeptics alike.

The case of the Pollock Twins continues to be one of the most discussed and analyzed cases in the study of reincarnation. It raises profound questions about the nature of life, death, and the possibility of life after death. For those who believe in reincarnation, the Pollock Twins offer compelling evidence of the continuity of consciousness and the potential for souls to return to the physical world. For skeptics, the case serves as an interesting study of human psychology and the powerful influence of belief and expectation.

Over the years, the story of the Pollock Twins has been featured in numerous books, documentaries, and articles. It remains a cornerstone case in the field of parapsychology and has inspired further research into the phenomena of past-life memories and reincarnation. The Pollock family, particularly John Pollock, remained steadfast in their belief that Joanna and Jacqueline had indeed returned to them in the form of Gillian and Jennifer, finding comfort in the idea that their daughters' souls had found a way back to their family.

Chapter 50: The Unsolved Murder of Bob Crane

The unsolved murder of Bob Crane is one of Hollywood's most enduring mysteries, shrouded in intrigue and speculation. Bob Crane, born on July 13, 1928, in Waterbury, Connecticut, gained fame as the star of the popular television sitcom "Hogan's Heroes," which aired from 1965 to 1971. The show, set in a German POW camp during World War II, showcased Crane's comedic talent and made him a household name. However, his life took a dark turn, leading to his brutal and still-unsolved murder on June 29, 1978, in Scottsdale, Arizona.

Bob Crane's career began in radio, where he became known as a charismatic and witty radio host in Los Angeles. His success in radio eventually led to opportunities in television, and he landed the role of Colonel Hogan in "Hogan's Heroes." The show was a significant hit, and Crane's portrayal of the quick-witted, resourceful POW leader made him a beloved figure in American households. However, as the show ended, Crane struggled to maintain his career's momentum, and his personal life began to unravel.

Crane's life off-screen was marked by a complex web of relationships and controversial behavior. He had a reputation for being a ladies' man and had a proclivity for videotaping his sexual encounters, a hobby that would later play a crucial role in the investigation of his murder. Crane often collaborated with John Henry Carpenter, a video equipment sales manager who became his close friend and accomplice in his sexual exploits. The two men would often lure women into Crane's apartment, where they filmed their activities. This aspect of Crane's life, kept hidden from the public eye, would eventually come under intense scrutiny following his death.

On the morning of June 29, 1978, Crane was found bludgeoned to death in his Scottsdale apartment. His body was discovered by Victoria Ann Berry, his co-star in a play they were performing at the time. Crane had been struck multiple times in the head with a blunt object, and an electrical cord was wrapped around his neck. The crime scene was gruesome, with blood splattered throughout the bedroom. Despite the violent nature of the crime, there were no signs of forced entry, suggesting that Crane may have known his killer.

The investigation into Crane's murder quickly focused on his friend John Henry Carpenter. Carpenter had been in Scottsdale visiting Crane at the time of the murder and had spent the previous evening with him. Witnesses reported seeing Carpenter's rental car near Crane's apartment on the night of the murder. Additionally, traces of blood were found in Carpenter's rental car, which investigators believed could be linked to the crime scene. However, forensic technology at the time was not advanced enough to definitively match the blood to Crane, and Carpenter maintained his innocence, insisting he had nothing to do with the murder.

Despite the circumstantial evidence against Carpenter, the case against him remained weak. In 1992, fourteen years after the murder, advancements in DNA testing prompted authorities to reopen the case. DNA analysis was performed on the blood samples found in Carpenter's rental car, but the results were inconclusive. Nevertheless, Carpenter was arrested and charged with Crane's murder. The trial, which took place in 1994, attracted significant media attention and was closely followed by the public.

During the trial, the prosecution argued that Carpenter had killed Crane out of jealousy and anger. They presented evidence of Carpenter's obsession with Crane and his declining mental state. The defense, however, countered that the evidence was purely circumstantial and did not definitively place Carpenter at the scene of the crime. The lack of concrete forensic evidence, combined with the absence of a clear motive, led to Carpenter's acquittal. The jury concluded that there was reasonable doubt regarding Carpenter's guilt, and he was released.

The acquittal did little to quell the speculation and theories surrounding Bob Crane's murder. Numerous theories have been proposed over the years, ranging from jealous lovers to organized crime involvement. Some believe that Crane's penchant for videotaping his sexual encounters may have led to his murder, possibly by someone who felt threatened by the potential exposure of the tapes. Others suggest that Crane's involvement with Carpenter and their activities may have attracted the attention of dangerous individuals.

One of the more compelling theories involves Carpenter's possible connection to the crime. Despite his acquittal, many believe that Carpenter had the motive and opportunity to kill Crane. Their close relationship, combined with Carpenter's presence in Scottsdale at the time of the murder, raises significant questions. Additionally, the blood evidence, although inconclusive, adds a layer of suspicion. Carpenter's behavior following the murder, including his inconsistent statements and erratic actions, has also fueled speculation about his involvement.

Another theory posits that Crane may have been killed by a jealous lover or someone associated with one of the women he filmed. Crane's promiscuous lifestyle and the secret recordings he made could have created enemies who felt betrayed or exposed. This theory suggests that Crane's murder was a crime of passion, committed by someone who felt they had been wronged by him. The brutal nature of the attack, with multiple blows to the head, supports the idea of a crime driven by intense emotion.

The involvement of organized crime has also been suggested, though there is little concrete evidence to support this theory. Some speculate that Crane's activities, particularly his videotaping, may have intersected with criminal elements who wanted to silence him. This theory, while less substantiated, adds another layer of complexity to the case.

Despite the various theories and extensive investigation, the murder of Bob Crane remains officially unsolved. The case has been the subject of numerous books, documentaries, and even a feature film, "Auto Focus," which delves into Crane's life and the circumstances surrounding his death. The enduring fascination with the case is a testament to the enigmatic nature of Crane's murder and the many unanswered questions that persist.

Forensic advancements continue to offer hope that new evidence might one day emerge to solve the case. Cold case investigators periodically review the evidence, and there remains a possibility that future developments in DNA technology or a new witness could finally bring closure to the case. Until then, the murder of Bob Crane remains one of Hollywood's most notorious and perplexing unsolved mysteries, a story marked by fame, scandal, and a tragic, violent end.

The unsolved murder of Bob Crane stands as a haunting reminder of the darker side of Hollywood's glamour and the complexities of human behavior. It highlights the challenges faced by investigators in solving crimes involving high-profile individuals and the limitations of forensic science in the late 20th century. Crane's life and death continue to captivate the public imagination, ensuring that his story remains a poignant chapter in the annals of true crime history.

Epilogue

As we conclude our exploration of "The Historical Forensic Files: Unsolved Cases Through Time," we find ourselves standing at the intersection of history and mystery. Each case we have examined offers a glimpse into moments of profound uncertainty, where the limits of human understanding are tested and the truth remains elusive. These stories, spanning centuries and continents, remind us of the complexity of the human condition and the enduring nature of unanswered questions.

The cases presented here are not merely historical curiosities or puzzles for the curious mind. They are, at their core, reflections of the real lives affected—victims, families, communities, and sometimes entire societies. Behind every unsolved case lies a tapestry of emotions, ranging from grief and fear to frustration and hope. The absence of closure leaves a lingering void, a space where speculation and myth often take root, sometimes obscuring the reality of the individuals involved.

Despite the advancements in forensic science and technology, which have solved many once-mysterious cases, there are still enigmas that defy explanation. DNA analysis, digital forensics, and other modern tools offer new hope, yet they are not infallible. In some instances, critical evidence is lost to time, while in others, the truth is buried under layers of human error, bias, or simply the chaotic nature of life itself.

But perhaps it is this very uncertainty that continues to draw us to these stories. The unsolved case represents a space where the imagination can roam, where the narrative is not fully closed. It challenges our perceptions of certainty and justice, inviting us to question and to seek answers, even when they may never be found.

As we close this book, we acknowledge that these mysteries may never be fully resolved. However, the pursuit of truth is itself a vital endeavor. It is a testament to our enduring curiosity and our desire to understand the world around us. Each unsolved case is a reminder of the fragile line between knowledge and the unknown, and the enduring human spirit that drives us to seek understanding.

In this pursuit, we honor not only the victims of these mysteries but also the countless investigators, journalists, and ordinary citizens who continue to seek the truth. Their dedication keeps these cases alive in our collective memory, ensuring that the search for answers continues.

The journey through the historical forensic files may come to an end here, but the stories remain open, inviting future generations to revisit and perhaps, one day, solve the enigmas that have long perplexed us. As we look to the future, we do so with the understanding that the quest for truth is never truly over, and the mystery, as it always has, endures.

The End.

www.ingramcontent.com/pod-product-compliance
Lightning Source LLC
Chambersburg PA
CBHW020334160726
47992CB00004B/1845